Water Garden Plants *for* Canada

Alison Beck

Lone Pine Publishing

The Publisher: Lone Pine Publishing
10145 – 81 Avenue   1808 B Street NW, Suite 140
Edmonton, AB, Canada T6E 1W9   Auburn, WA, USA 98001
Website: www.lonepinepublishing.com

Library and Archives Canada Cataloguing in Publication
Beck, Alison, 1971-
   Water garden plants for Canada / Alison Beck.

ISBN-13: 978-1-55105-465-0
ISBN-10: 1-55105-465-5

     1. Aquatic plants--Canada. 2. Water gardens--Canada.
I. Title.

SB423.B42 2005   635.9'674'0971   C2005-900101-1

Editorial Director: Nancy Foulds
Project Editor: Gary Whyte
Editorial: Gary Whyte, Rachelle Delaney
Photo Coordination: Don Williamson, Heather Markham, Alison Beck
Illustrations Coordination: Carol Woo
Production Manager: Gene Longson
Book Design, Layout & Production: Heather Markham
Image Editing & Production Support: Curtis Pillipow, Trina Koscielnuk, Elliot Engley
Cover Design: Gerry Dotto
Scanning & Digital Film: Elite Lithographers Co.

Photographic Credits: See p. 288 for complete list of photographers.

Cover photograph: Saxon Holt

Hardiness map information taken from *The Atlas of Canada* (http://atlas.gc.ca) © 2004. Her Majesty the Queen in Right of Canada with permission from Natural Resources Canada.

This book is not intended as a 'how-to' guide on eating garden plants. No plant or plant extract should be consumed unless you are certain of its identity and toxicity and of your potential for allergic reactions.

We acknowledge the financial support of the Government of Canada through the Book Publishing Industry Development Program (BPIDP) for our publishing activities.

PC: P1

Contents

Acknowledgements

I WOULD LIKE TO THANK the following for their invaluable contributions to *Water Garden Plants for Canada:* Mike Bauer, Liza Fleming, John Bueglas and Henry and Gillian van Elst all took time to review the text and offer advice. The Lone Pine Publishing team, especially Heather Markham in production, used its talent and expertise to make this most beautiful and unique book. Thanks to all who contributed photos and allowed us to photograph their water gardens. I hope this inspires Canadian gardeners everywhere to discover the art of water gardening.

The Plants at a Glance

Pictorial Guide in Alphabetical Order

Anacheris p. 66	Angelica p. 68	Arrowhead p. 70	Astilbe p. 72
Bee Balm p. 74	Beech Fern p. 76	Birch p. 78	Bladderwort p. 80
Bleeding Heart p. 82	Bog Bean p. 84 / Bugbane p. 90	Brass Buttons p. 86 / Bugleweed p. 92	Buckler Fern p. 88 / Cabomba p. 94

Calla Lily
p. 96

Canadian Hemlock
p. 98

Cattail
p. 100

Cedar
p. 102

Chameleon Plant
p. 104

Club Rush
p. 106

Columbine
p. 108

Common Cotton Grass
p. 110

Corydalis
p. 112

Curled Pondweed
p. 114

Daylily
p. 116

Dogwood
p. 118

Duckweed
p. 120

Elephant Ears
p. 122

Flowering Fern
p. 130

Eupatorium
p. 124

Fairy Moss
p. 126

Floating Heart
p. 128

Flowering Rush
p. 132

Giant Arum
p. 136

Frogbit
p. 134

Goat's Beard
p. 138

Golden Club
p. 140

Gunnera
p. 142

Hardy Calla
p. 144

Horsetail
p. 146

Hosta
p. 148

Iris
p. 150

Jacob's Ladder
p. 152

Kaffir Lily
p. 154

Katsura-tree
p. 156

Lady Fern
p. 158

Lobelia
p. 164

Ligularia
p. 160

Lizard's Tail
p. 162

Loosestrife
p. 166

Lotus
p. 168

Lungwort
p. 172

Maidenhair Fern
p. 174

Manna Grass
p. 176

Maple
p. 178

Marsh Marigold
p. 180

Masterwort
p. 182

Meadow Rue
p. 184

Meadowsweet
p. 186

Monkey Flower
p. 188

Monkshood
p. 190

Mountain Laurel
p. 192

Obedient Plant
p. 194

Ornamental Rhubarb
p. 196

Ostrich Fern
p. 198

Papyrus
p. 200

Parrot Feather
p. 202

Pennywort
p. 204

Plume Poppy
p. 212

Periwinkle
p. 206

Pickerel Weed
p. 208

Pitcher Plant
p. 210

Primrose
p. 214

Rush
p. 220

Ribbon Grass
p. 216

Rodgersia
p. 218

Salvinia
p. 222

Sedge
p. 224

Shield Fern
p. 226

Silver Grass
p. 228

Spearwort
p. 230

Spike Rush
p. 232

Swamp Hibicus
p. 234

Sweet Flag
p. 236

Thalia
p. 238

Turtle Head
p. 240

Umbrella Plant
p. 242

Valerian
p. 244

Virginia Bluebells
p. 246

Water Forget-Me-Not
p. 248

Water Hyacinth
p. 250

Water Lettuce
p. 252

Water Lily
p. 254

Water Poppy
p. 258

Watercress
p. 260

Willow
p. 262

Wood Rush
p. 264

Yellow Pond Lily
p. 266

OTHER PLANTS TO CONSIDER

Butterwort
p. 268

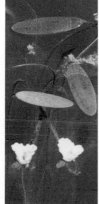

Cape Pondweed
p. 268

Hornwort
p. 270

Pondweed
p. 271

Tape Grass
p. 272

Water Soldier
p. 273

Yellow Wax-Bells
p. 275

Introduction

Water gardening has become increasingly popular with gardeners across Canada. The sight of ponds and waterfalls and the sound of running or trickling water are soothing balms in our increasingly hectic lives. Stopping beside a pond to greet your pet goldfish or koi, watch water gliders skate across the surface or see your first water lily bloom encourages you to slow down and take note of what is going on around you.

This book briefly discusses the initial steps to establishing a water garden—installing water features, learning the basics of maintenance and creating a balanced system. Its main purpose, though, is to provide instruction in the selection, planting locations and care of your water garden plants. This includes information about plant size, hardiness and preferred growing conditions.

The right plants turn a pond or other water feature into a water garden. They grow in and around your water feature, blending it into the surrounding garden. Creating a personal oasis is a matter of understanding your water garden plants and what they need to thrive.

Canada is geologically diverse, but its entire geography has been influenced—if not created—by the glaciers

of the last ice age. A multitude of river valleys wind through the drainage basins created when the glaciers melted and receded; their depths and widths are often much greater than seems necessary for today's water flows. The carvings of the glaciers are etched on ancient mountain ranges and wide flood-plains, and deposits of sand, rock and silt mark the glaciers' passage, unifying the country, despite its size.

Overall, Canada is a fantastic country in which to garden, though the cold winter weather in many regions does present some chal-lenges. A wealth of diverse growing conditions are found here—almost every imaginable gardening situa-tion short of tropical is experienced somewhere in the country.

The adjacent oceans significantly modify the climate on both the East Coast and the West Coast, resulting in more moderate winter tempera-tures and cooler summers, as well as fog, salty air and often thin, rocky, acidic soils. The warmer winters of the West Coast, in particular, allow for a far wider range of plants than anywhere else in Canada. Depending on the direction of the prevailing wind, precipitation and humidity are also typically increased. Pockets of sandy soil are common as well.

Warm summers and cold winters dominate in most of eastern and central Canada. The floodplains that border the St. Lawrence River are fer-tile and deep, and the climate is modified by their proximity to water. Gardeners on the Canadian Shield generally have acidic and fertile but rocky soils, whereas those living

Hardiness Zones Map

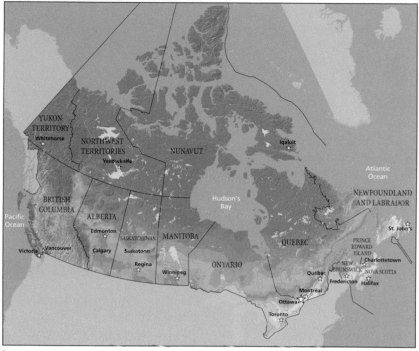

Plant Hardiness
Zones for Canada

| 0a | 0b | 1a | 1b | 2a | 2b | 3a | 3b | 4a |
| 4b | 5a | 5b | 6a | 6b | 7a | 7b | 8a | |

around Georgian Bay have sandy soils. Southern Ontario has mostly alkaline, less rocky soil and milder winters, thanks to the moderating effect of the Great Lakes.

The cold winters of the Prairies are hard on tender plants, but the sun-filled days of summer encourage plant growth. The soils can be clay, sand or loam, and they tend to be alkaline.

The Rocky Mountains provide unique challenges, with short, often dry summers and cold winters. The valleys between the mountains are often more temperate, and there is no shortage of gardeners to take advantage of the best the region has to offer.

The North, though sparsely populated, has its share of determined water gardeners. The varied geography shares many traits with adjacent areas farther south, such as the Rockies, the Prairies or the Canadian Shield, but typically with thin, acidic soils, low levels of precipitation, scattered permafrost and, of course, very cold winters and a short growing season. Native plants and those from similarly frosty regions elsewhere in the world dominate water gardens in this area.

Despite these regional characteristics and limitations, conditions can deviate greatly from garden to garden within a region. In addition to broad factors such as climate, season length and day length, the details of soil conditions, garden microclimates, light and heat influence your garden regardless of where you are in Canada, and they vary from garden to garden and even within each garden. Together, these details create the conditions unique to your own garden.

Canada is divided into hardiness zones based on climatic factors such as winter cold and season duration. Plants are then rated based on their abilities to survive the conditions in each zone. The system provides a good starting point, but it should not be the absolute word on whether

or not you choose to grow a plant. Very sheltered gardens may provide the conditions of a warmer zone. Summer heat may be more intense in one area than another, even if both are considered the same zone. If you want to grow plants that aren't listed as hardy for your area, consider using some of the strategies described elsewhere in this book for overwintering tender water garden plants; you can always try something different next year if this year's experiment doesn't work out. I always try to make sure 80–90% of my plants are tried and true hardy. The other 10–20% can be experiments.

Water gardening should be fun. Having a pond opens up a huge variety of possible plants for all Canadian gardeners. Be adventurous and create a unique and beautiful water feature that reflects your own personality and the things that you like best in the garden.

West Nile Virus has many people fearful of the increased mosquito population they suspect may come along with their new ponds. Fortunately, these fears can be laid to rest. Mosquitoes prefer to breed in still water—if you keep your circulation system and waterfall flowing, mosquitoes will avoid laying their eggs, and their larvae will not survive. Also, fish are avaricious devourers of insects, including any mosquito eggs or larvae that might find their way into your pond. It has even been suggested that a healthy pond with a good circulation system and healthy fish will actually reduce the local mosquito population.

Pond Basics

TREMENDOUS ADVANCES HAVE been made in pond technology in the past few years. What at one time could quickly become a maintenance nightmare is now a truly enjoyable and environmentally friendly hobby. New products and techniques that work with nature plus a greater understanding of what a pond needs to establish a balanced system have made pond ownership simpler than ever.

Planning

Water features vary greatly in style and form. They can be raised above the ground or sunk below. They can be large enough to fill your whole yard or small enough to fit in a half-barrel. Water features are considered formal or informal, but they can have a mixture of both kinds of characteristics. Formal ponds tend to be symmetrical in shape. Their plantings reflect this symmetry—usually plants that are neat in habit—and don't obscure the pond margins, letting the water feature stand out in the landscape. Informal ponds, more often asymmetrical or irregular in form, attempt to imitate natural water environments with plantings that hide edges and blend features into the surrounding landscape.

Rules and Regulations

Before you start planning a pond, check with your local bylaw department to see what rules and requirements are in place regarding ponds. As open sources of water, ponds over a certain size may require specific fencing arrangements and you may need a permit. These rules differ widely from community to community.

Bog gardens can include many attractive features.

When choosing a water feature for your garden, consider the style of your existing garden and create one that will complement both your garden and your home.

Once you've decided on the style of pond, you should consider where the pond should go and how big it should be, to make the best use of your available space.

Pond Location

One of your most important decisions involves picking the right spot for your pond. A good location will provide the best growing conditions for your plants and can even reduce pond maintenance.

First and foremost, you should consider light availability. Most pond plants, particularly flowering ones, need at least six hours of direct sunlight to perform their best. Submerged plants, too, can best outcompete algae if they receive plenty of light. Buildings, large trees and other large objects can reduce the amount of direct light significantly, and the amount of shade can vary dramatically from season to season. Trees also drop leaves into the pond, producing gases as they decompose that are harmful to fish, amphibians and other pond dwellers. Remove leaves from the pond before they have a chance to sink and decompose, either by using a net or by installing a skimmer when you build your pond. The roots of large trees can make digging difficult, and chopping through too many roots can be bad for the tree. Roots can also cause future problems if they continue to grow after your pond is installed. In most cases, it is best to choose a sunny, open area for your pond. However, many of the plants we prefer to grow around our ponds appreciate some afternoon shade, which you can get by strategically planting small trees and shrubs.

An open area is usually the best site for a pond, but such a location may also be exposed and windy, and this can increase evaporation from the pond's surface and may lead to some emergent plants being damaged by the movement of the lapping water. Again, a good solution is to plant small trees and shrubs, particularly on the pond's windward side. Be sure that any windbreak allows air to flow through it, however. A solid windbreak, such as a fence or a stone wall, creates turbulence on the leeward side, exacerbating the problem, whereas a porous windbreak reduces the flow without creating turbulence.

A pond may look natural when placed in a hollow or low spot in your garden, but siting a pond here can lead to higher maintenance. Because water naturally drains to the lowest spot, your pond may overflow, and any excess fertilizers used on lawns will likely wash into the pond, creating problems with algae bloom. A better idea is to site the pond just above the lowest spot and create a bog garden in the low area or designate it as the pond overflow area. Plant it with species that don't mind periodic inundation.

Additional problems with excessive water collection can include water getting under the liner and lifting it away from the ground, dirt washing away from the sides or from underneath your pond, and your pond hardware (such as skimmer boxes and waterfall filters) tearing away from the pond liner if the soil supporting the hardware washes away. If a low spot is your only choice of location, be sure to install good drainage beneath the pond to avoid these problems.

Because cold air tends to accumulate in low spots, you may find that late and early frosts unexpectedly damage or kill plants in spring or fall. Once again, the solution is to site the pond just a bit farther up any natural slope.

Unfortunately, not all of our gardens have an ideal location for a pond, but that doesn't mean you shouldn't have one. It just means you need to choose your plants more carefully. Some water garden plants prefer moist, shady areas, including a few shade-tolerant oxygenators.

Using a natural slope

Others grow well in the moving water created by the wind in an exposed area, and some won't be damaged by the additional frosts that often plague low spots. Everyone can have a pond to enjoy, and every pond can be unique.

Another important consideration is where you will be in relation to your pond. Situate your pond near a deck or patio or plan a sitting area next to your pond so you can enjoy it as much as possible. It is nice to have the pond clearly visible from indoor sitting areas, too. That way, you can enjoy pond-watching when the weather isn't nice enough to be

in the garden. When deciding where to put features such as waterfalls and where to locate short plants and tall plants, consider what you will want to see from the different viewing locations you have in mind. Although many people will want their pond's features to be enjoyed from many locations, others may prefer to add a bit of mystery with different vantage points offering different experiences, and some gardeners may even want to put their pond into its own garden 'room.'

If you are planning a waterfall or want a stream to flow into your pond, remember that water always flows downhill, so work with the contours of your yard if you can. Otherwise you will need to move a lot of soil around. Use the soil you excavate when digging the pond to create a berm for a waterfall, but be sure it has gentle slopes and isn't too tall or it could wind up looking more like a volcano than a natural part of the landscape.

It's a good idea to draft a scale drawing of the part of the yard where your pond will be, using graph paper or a computer program. This will help you create a design that fits and works for you before you start digging or buying parts. Be sure to include sitting areas and adjacent planting areas as well as connection points for water and electricity. If you intend to use a flexible liner, you can also plan for shelves, sloping beaches, planting pockets and similar features to accommodate the needs of the plants you would like to grow. Having a drawing will also make it easier to discuss your project with parts suppliers and anyone else you go to for assistance.

Pond Size

When designing a pond, bear in mind that you will probably get the most satisfaction from it if you make it as big as your space and budget will allow. One of the comments frequently made by first-time pond owners is that they wished they had started with a bigger pond. The size of the pond determines how many plants and fish your pond can accommodate and influences water temperature fluctuations.

Many water garden plants require quite a bit of space, and many are of rather rampant growth habits. The larger the pond, the more varieties of plants we can include, and the less often we will have to divide them, trim them back or scoop them out.

The larger the volume of water, the longer the pond will take to heat up or cool down. Consistent water temperatures provide better growing conditions for your plants and better living conditions for your fish, both of which fare poorly when water temperatures change too quickly. Widely fluctuating water temperatures can also be detrimental to the populations of beneficial bacteria and can encourage algae bloom.

Pond size is determined by both surface area and depth, which usually vary across the pond. The surface area will be dependent on the amount of space you have and want to devote to the pond. Regardless of whether your pond is 90 cm (3') or 9 m (30') across, its depth should probably be 45–75 cm (18–30"),

Call Before You Dig
As with any project where you will be digging pits or holes, call the utility company to find out where your service lines are buried. Most utility companies have a locator service and will come to your house to let you know where gas, power, sewer and any other service lines are located. Check your local blue pages or call your utility company for more information.

with small ponds at the shallow end of the range and large ponds at the deep end. Depths in this range are adequate to shelter small fish from many predators. In addition, these depths permit only partial winter freezing in most Canadian gardens and also allow the water to warm up fairly quickly in spring but without frequent extreme temperature fluctuations. In the coldest parts of Canada, a deeper area should be incorporated into the pond to successfully overwinter fish. Koi, in particular, do best in water at least 90 cm (3') or even 1.8 m (6') deep.

Building Your Pond

You've picked your spot and have a pretty solid idea of how you want the pond to look. The final thing to consider is which of various construction methods to use. A wide variety of materials are available for building ponds, each with their own advantages and disadvantages. From simple preformed ponds that require little more than a shovel to install to reinforced concrete ponds that require an entire construction crew, the possibilities are endless. A quick look at the pros and cons of each method can help you decide on the construction method that best fits your budget, your style and your needs.

Liners

Unless you have a heavy clay soil that drains very, very slowly, you will need to line your pond to keep the water where you want it. Concrete, preformed liners and flexible liners are the most common choices.

Because of its unlimited possibilities for size and shape, as well as a potential for high durability, concrete was once the most popular way to line a pond. This approach has now fallen out of favour for home gardens, because concrete is time-, labour- and skill-intensive, and it doesn't last well if poorly made. Today, concrete is most commonly used in large projects, such as those in public parks, botanical gardens and similar places, where it is installed by skilled contractors.

Preformed liners may be rigid or semi-rigid; rigid liners are made of fibreglass or reinforced plastic and semi-rigid liners are made of molded plastic. Preformed liners are convenient, easy to repair and come in a variety of shapes, both formal and informal. They are particularly useful for creating formal and raised ponds and are good for use on slopes. However, they are not suitable for keeping koi or for overwintering fish of any kind. Also, the hole into which you fit a preformed liner must be lined with at least 10 cm (4") of sand, and it must be dug to match the liner exactly. Only fairly small liner sizes are available, and cracking can occur if the support on the sides is insufficient. Improper installation can also lead to frost heaving during the winter, which requires the pond to be re-leveled in spring.

Flexible liners offer an almost unlimited range of sizes and shapes for your pond because pieces of liner can be joined together if necessary. They are made in a variety of materials, of which PVC (polyvinyl chloride) and EPDM (ethylene propylene diene monomer) are the most common and fairly comparable pricewise. PVC can degrade when

Hiring an Installer

Although installing a pond isn't complicated, it can be hard work. The bigger the pond, the more digging will be required and the more time it will take. If you are unable or would prefer not to construct the pond yourself, there are a few things to ask potential contractors before hiring. Find out how many ponds they have installed and how long they have been doing this kind of work. Ask to see photos of ponds they have installed to make sure the kinds of ponds they create are in the style you envision for your yard. Adding a pond is a large investment, so you want to be sure that you get the pond you want. Ask if they guarantee their work and for how long. Always ask for references from previous clients, and even ask to meet previous clients—see if you can visit their ponds. Finally, be sure the contractor is insured. Insurance protects you from lawsuits should any personal injuries occur while the job is underway.

pond liners

submersible pumps

For very large projects, polyethylene or polypropylene liners are often used because they are available in pieces up to 2800 m^2 (30,000 ft^2). A forklift or tractor is mandatory to move a liner of this size.

Pumps and Filters

Pumps are used to circulate water through the pond. They oxygenate the water, operate a fountain or move water to the top of a waterfall or stream and are often used in conjunction with a filtration system. Ideally, your pump and filtration system should be allowed to operate 24 hours per day, and as a general rule, its capacity should be sufficient to process at least half the water feature's contents every hour, with an even higher capacity for ponds in full sun or with koi.

External pumps are located outside of the pond and are generally used to move high volumes of water. Usually only used in large installations, they are noisy, can overheat if enclosed to reduce noise and may run dry if situated above the water line and a power interruption occurs.

Submersible pumps are located in the pond. The hum they make is muffled by the water. A variety of sizes are available, capable of moving water through just about any size of garden pond. Most are fitted with prefilters that prevent large debris from entering the pump and clogging it. Watch for excessive build-up of debris on the prefilter because this can reduce the water flow enough for the pump to run dry. The prefilter should allow algae and

exposed to sunlight and it develops leaks most easily. PVC lasts for 10 to 20 years. EPDM is more flexible and durable than PVC, and it holds up well to climate extremes. EPDM lasts 20–40 years. The standard for North American ponds is considered to be 45 mil EPDM liners. This type of liner is heavy: a 6–7.5 m (20 x 25') EPDM liner weighs about 70 kg (150 lbs.) Both PVC and EPDM last longest if they are protected from sunlight with a layer of rocks and gravel. Both types of flexible liner can be repaired when punctured. The main drawbacks of flexible liners are that the pieces can be awkward and heavy to handle and they must be folded to fit into the shape of the pond, although a covering of rocks and gravel will hide the folds.

small debris to pass through to the filter, reducing the build-up on the prefilter.

A filtration system is used to remove unwanted matter, such as floating or decomposing debris, algae or excess nutrients, from the pond. Once the debris settles it will not be eliminated by the filter. All commercial filters perform both mechanical and a biological functions. A mechanical filter collects physical debris for convenient removal and the biological filter eliminates excess nutrients from the water. When choosing filters, be sure to take into account their ease of servicing as well as their maximum flow rate. Never exceed the maximum flow rate recommended by the manufacturer. If water flows too quickly through the filter it will not filter effectively and can overflow.

One common mechanical filter is a skimmer-style filter. It has a wide opening at water level and is attached to the side of the pond; some models have a pump incorporated into the same housing. As the pump draws the water through the filter, floating leaves, mosquito larvae, algae and other surface debris are trapped in the filter, letting only the water pass through to the pump, and then typically to a biological filter. The skimmer-style filter only collects debris that is at or near the surface of the pond. The net or basket that collects debris has to be cleaned out regularly, but unless a lot of debris falls into your pond it will not have to be cleared out very frequently.

The biological filter contains layers or bags of a medium that supports a population of beneficial bacteria. The bacteria consume the excess nutrients that are produced in your pond, such as the nutrients from fish wastes. It keeps nutrient levels safe for fish and reduces the amount available for algae to consume. Biological filters need to be fairly large in order to be effective, and they are often designed with a waterfall flowing out of the top. For best water circulation, the water should usually re-enter the pond at the point most distant from the skimmer or pump intake.

A UV clarifier unit added to the filtration system uses ultraviolet light to kill water-borne algae as it passes through. Units made for pond use are weaker than the UV

pond filter

centrifugal pumps & telescoping tubes

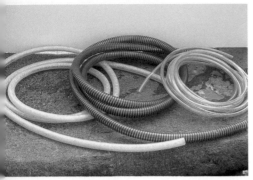

various tubing

front: waterfall/filters; back: pond skimmers

pond lights

enough to destroy single-cell algae. Spring is the best time for bulb replacement; this is when you want the unit to be at its peak efficiency. A UV filter may not be required at all. Algae generally flourishes in the spring then subsides as plant life in your pond begins to grow more vigorously. A UV filter can always be added later if absolutely necessary.

Barley straw mats or pellets can also be added to the pond system to further reduce algae, but results usually take one or two months. The decay of barley straw creates a substance (hydrogen peroxide) that is toxic to algae but will not harm your plants or fish. Because sunlight and sufficient dissolved oxygen are essential to the formation of this substance, the filter immediately before the waterfall is a good place to keep the straw.

Several companies have started producing complete pond kits that come with clear instructions and all the parts you need to build a pond. They are available for both flexible and preformed liner ponds. Many books that explain the detailed process of installing a pond are available, and expert advice is almost always available at nurseries and garden centres that sell pond equipment and supplies. Independent suppliers that specialize in pond supplies offer some of the best experience and advice.

Especially if you have fish, consider getting a pond water-testing kit so that you can verify that the various nutrients and other substances dissolved in the water remain within appropriate ranges.

sterilizers designed for killing bacteria and viruses in swimming pools or drinking water and should not harm other pond life. Bulbs should be replaced every 12 months to ensure they are burning brightly

The Pond Ecosystem

Ponds of all shapes and sizes are created using the same basic parts, but it takes more than these parts to build a balanced, algae-free pond. A balanced system will ensure an organic water garden that requires only minimal ongoing maintenance. A balance is achieved when the nutrients produced equal the nutrients consumed by the system and when sufficient oxygen remains dissolved in the water to support the bacteria, fish, plants and other life in your pond.

The components that work together to balance the pond ecosystem are the circulation and filtration system, rocks and gravel, plants, fish and bacteria. When working effectively together, they keep algae under control and mosquitoes to a minimum and prevent the water from becoming stagnant and smelly. With a balanced system, the bulk of the maintenance consists of regularly clearing debris out of the skimmer basket, trimming off dying leaves and pruning back some of the more vigorous plants.

The main purpose of the circulation system is to cycle the water through the pond to keep it from becoming stagnant. It also drives the water through a filtration system, which removes floating matter, such as fallen leaves and insect larvae, and excess nutrients that can lead to algae growth.

Even a small or gently flowing waterfall will, in addition to its aesthetic appeal, have the added benefit of adding oxygen to the water, which is especially important in warm weather and at night. Warm water holds less oxygen, and at night plants don't release it. Fish and beneficial bacteria suffer in an oxygen-deprived pond, and having sufficient oxygen dissolved in your pond is one of the most vital factors in preventing unpleasant odours.

Lining your pond with rocks and gravel not only gives your pond an attractive, natural appearance, but these materials are an important part of the system. Beneficial aerobic bacteria flourish on the surfaces of the rocks, consuming excess nutrients and breaking down debris that accumulates at the bottom of the pond. These surfaces are also appreciated by fish, such as koi, that enjoy browsing through the gravel for food and nibbling algae off the rocks. Rocks can also provide shade, shelter and hiding places from predators for your fish, frogs, snails and any other small wildlife that call your pond home. However, it is possible for oxygen-starved anaerobic or dead spots to occur in the gravel, and gravel can make finding leaks more difficult.

Fish are more than just fun to watch. They eat mosquito eggs and larvae as well as other insects that land on the water's surface, and they nibble submerged oxygenators, keeping them pruned back and their growth under control. Many fish also eat algae.

Plants are a vital component in the pond. When appropriately chosen and situated, they consume excess nutrients, release oxygen into the water and provide shade and shelter—and look good doing it.

Every pond has its own characteristics and every situation is unique. Not every pond requires a filtration system. Many ponds, with the right balance of sunlight, plants, aquatic life, and water depth, volume and circulation, are fine on their own.

A newly installed pond won't become an instant ecosystem. It takes time for plants to fill in, bacteria to flourish and everything to settle into its own rhythm. Give your pond the time it needs, but keep an eye open for serious problems and deal with them in the least invasive way possible. Eventually, over the summer, you'll find your pond has become the low-maintenance delight you originally had in mind.

Water Garden Plants

INCLUDING A POND in your garden does more than just introduce water. My motivation for water gardening has always been to open up new possibilities for the types of plants I can grow. Not only can plants be introduced to the pond itself, but you can create moist areas around the pond where a wide variety of species can thrive, including ones that you may not have had success with in the past because you just couldn't keep the soil moist enough. Or you may even want to create a bog garden on its own.

Aquatic plants are grouped into categories based loosely on their growth habits and where in the water they grow: submerged, floating, emergent or marginal, bog and pondside. Each of these groups has a different role in the water garden, and some plants span two or more categories.

Submerged plants can be divided into two basic types: oxygenators, which are vital to sustaining a healthy pond, and other species that simply grow underwater. Submerged oxygenators usually have fine, feathery underwater foliage, but some kinds also produce leaves

Curled pondweed is a submerged oxygenating perennial.

Water lily is a rooted floater.

Fish love to eat free-floating duckweed.

that float on the water's surface. Some oxygenators float freely in the water and have no roots at all. If they do have roots, they use them more for anchoring than for feeding. Like many other pond plants, oxygenators provide shade, shelter and food for fish and small water dwellers of other kinds. What sets oxygenators apart from other submerged plants, however, is that they are especially known for releasing oxygen into the water (during the day, when they are actively growing) and for competing with algae for the excess nutrients in the water, thereby reducing the amount of green slime that grows in your pond.

By using more than one type of submerged oxygenator in a pond, you can create a varied underwater landscape of different textures and shades of green. These plants are often sold in bundles or bunches. To control algae growth, a rough guide is to plant 5–20 bunches per m² (1–2 bunches for every 1–2 ft²) of pond surface area. You may find you

have to trim some of the plants back in summer as they fill in.

Many submerged plants that do not consume excess nutrients to the same extent as oxygenators are also welcome in our ponds because they are attractive and sometimes have flowers. They can also provide shelter and snacks for fish.

Floating plants fall into two categories: those that are free-floating and those that are rooted in the pond bottom but have leaves that float on the water's surface. Although many of these plants are grown primarily for their ornamental leaves and flowers, they also play an important role in reducing algae bloom and reducing temperature fluctuations by shading the surface of the water. Ideally, about 60% of the water's surface should be covered with floating leaves. This coverage provides shade without blocking so much light that your submerged oxygenating plants fail to thrive. Also, keeping some of the water surface exposed encourages

Sweet flag is a marginal aquatic perennial.

Pond Wildlife

Water gardens seem to have an unlimited ability to attract wildlife. Beyond the plant and fish introductions we make to our ponds, we find a wealth of expected and unexpected visitors and inhabitants. Birds come to drink, bathe and sometimes feed. Frogs, salamanders and toads seek out the water; each spring a batch of wriggling tadpoles hatches, and those not devoured are fascinating to watch as they slowly transform into adults. A variety of insects also takes up residence. Many of them are beneficial, eating either unwanted insects or the decomposing matter that inevitably accumulates in the pond. A water feature is an open invitation for local wildlife to call your garden home.

Marsh marigold is a marginal plant.

Pitcher plant, a carnivorous bog perennial

Add interest to the pondside garden with different heights and colours.

oxygen exchange and allows toxic gases to escape more easily.

Emergent and **marginal** plants are similar, differing mostly in the depth of the water in which they grow. Both can be loosely defined as plants that have their roots underwater and their stems, leaves and flowers above the water's surface. Marginals, which tend to grow in shallower water than emergents, may even be able to grow in moist soil around the pond rather than in the water. The main purpose of emergents and marginals is ornamental, but they do provide some shade and shelter for fish, frogs and other pond dwellers, and their flowers and seeds can provide food for desirable insects and birds.

True **bog** plants grow in waterlogged, acidic soil and typically get most or all of their nutrients from sources other than the soil, often by consuming insects. From a pond perspective, bog plants are species that thrive in wet soil. Some plants in this category may not mind being waterlogged periodically—such as during a period of heavy rain or during a spring melt—but they prefer a less waterlogged soil for the majority of the year.

Pondside plants form the transition between pond plantings and the rest of the garden. This category is often considered to consist of plants that like moist but well-drained soil. However, unless the liner is leaking or a lot of splashing occurs, most of our home ponds actually release very little water into the surrounding soil, so this plant group can be expanded to include any species that looks good next to a pond, even if it requires relatively dry soil.

Using a variety of plants from each category will help you create a pond with a natural appearance that provides interest and draws attention year-round with features such as flowers, colourful foliage and interesting forms. As with any gardening, however, it is important to put the right plant in the right location. Before planting, consider the expected mature size of all the plants you plan to include, and make sure you will have sufficient space for them in succeeding years, particularly with trees, shrubs and long-lived perennials. Annuals and short-lived perennials can be used to fill any awkward spaces in the meantime. Also, select plants that will grow well with the amount of light your garden provides and the type of soil in your garden. Be prepared to alter your plantings over time—sunny spots are likely to shade over as trees and large shrubs mature, and some plants will die or become too diseased or pest-ridden.

Purchasing Plants

Many garden centres now carry a selection of water garden plants. Specialty nurseries also exist in some localities, and a lot of them offer mail-order service. When purchasing water garden plants, as with any plants, choose the healthiest specimens you can find. Once you

familiarize yourself with the many possible water garden plants, you will have a good idea of what healthy plants look like. Check the leaves for pests and diseases and avoid plants with disfigured growth.

The propagation methods for water garden plants are similar to those used for other plants. Some plants can be started from seed, and many gardeners take an active interest in propagating plants this way. However, perennials grown from seed can take many years to mature. Therefore, it is often easiest to purchase plants or get divisions from friends and neighbours who have ponds, especially if you are just starting out in water gardening. Then, if you are interested in seeding and other methods of propagation, you can try it knowing that your pond will not suffer from a lack of plants while you wait for your young plants to mature. Refer to the section on propagation in this book for more information.

Planting

The plants that you grow in your pond have slightly different requirements than those planted around the pond or elsewhere in the garden. For example, the soil should be fertile but should not leach excess nutrients into the water. Also, large containers can be heavy and awkward to lift once they are saturated with water and the plants are mature. A few simple steps taken at planting time will make long-term plant maintenance much simpler.

Containers

The wide variety of containers suitable for water gardening are generally available where you buy your water garden plants. Choose containers that are wider than they are tall because most water garden plants have wide-spreading root systems. Using deeper pots isn't necessary and just makes the pots heavy to lift. Whatever their design, your containers should also allow water and gases to flow in and out of the pot while keeping the soil in. Plastic pots are most commonly used in the pond because they are inexpensive, lightweight and durable and don't leach damaging chemicals into the water.

Underwater Planting Beds

Many water gardeners are making underwater planting beds an integral part of their water gardens. When the pond is first dug, pockets and hollows are created for planting. The flexible liner is layed over these, creating a larger planting area than can be achieved with containers. With the liner in place, but before adding water, you can fill these areas with wet soil mix or pea gravel, add plants and then top the soil with rocks and gravel.

Some debate has arisen regarding the merits of planting water garden plants in containers versus planting directly into the pond. Both methods have their good and bad points (see chart, below).

You can enjoy the best of both worlds by using a combination of direct planting and container growing. Plant oxygenators and some of the submerged, emergent and marginal plants with less vigorous root systems directly in the pond. Then use containers for plants with vigorous root systems or those you will have to divide often or remove for winter. To hide unsightly containers from view, tuck them into pockets in the rocks and gravel.

Direct planting
- gives the pond a more natural appearance
- allows the roots to spread out, encouraging better use of water-borne nutrients
- permits the plants to grow larger, bloom better and be more resistant to problems
- increases the amount of time until division is required
- may allow vigorous plant roots to puncture the liner
- makes for harder removal of plants for division, rearrangement or overwintering when water is in the pond
- can spread soil throughout the pond when adding or removing plants unless you plant in pea gravel
- can require greater vigilance in dealing with invasive plants

Containers
- allow easy removal from the pond for plant division, maintenance or pest treatment
- facilitate the adjustment of depth underwater when introducing new plants or removing them in fall
- keep the soil contained, preventing discolouration of the water
- can be outgrown quickly, resulting in a need for frequent division or repotting
- can be messy if they get knocked over
- are usually not very attractive sitting in the pond, unless rocks are used to disguise them

Soil

Regardless of your chosen method of planting, you need the right soil mix. For pond plants, we usually recommend a heavy, loamy soil. Garden soil with a high clay content is a good choice—we will refer to it as a loamy pond mix throughout this book. Sandy soil is often too poor in nutrients to support vigorous water plant growth. If your local soil isn't appropriate, you can get bags of suitable soil at most garden centres that sell water plants.

Before you use garden soil in your pond, either in containers or for direct planting, first remove all the bits that will rise up and float on the surface of your pond. To do this, simply shovel the soil into a large container (such as a garbage can) and stir it thoroughly as you add enough water to float all the bits of light organic matter, then scoop them off.

The peat-based mixes that are commonly recommended for land-based container plants are not appropriate for water garden containers for several reasons. Peat tends to float, it can discolour the water and it is too acidic for most water garden plants, except for true bog plants and a few others.

Plants grown next to your pond can have a wide variety of soil needs. In general, an average to fertile soil with plenty of organic matter mixed in will be suitable. Organic matter such as compost helps the soil stay moist but not wet. Many pondside plants tolerate periodic flooding, but most of them don't like to grow in constantly soggy soil. Check the accounts in this book for each plant's specific soil requirements.

Having the correct soil and water acidity is part of ensuring a healthy water garden. Acidity is measured using the pH scale, which goes from zero to 14. Seven means neutral, smaller numbers indicate greater acidity, and higher numbers mark more basic or alkaline soil or water. Equipment and supplies for measuring pH and instructions for their use are available at garden centres.

Soil pH is of greater concern for pondside plants than for water plants. Soil pH affects what nutrients are available to the plants and other factors related to their health. Most pondside plants prefer a neutral to acidic soil, whereas most bog plants are adapted to an acidic or very acidic soil (pH of 4–5). Leaching by water and heavy use of fertilizers are common causes of acidic soil. Lime can be used to reduce soil acidity; the soil composition determines how much to use. Generally, though, soil pH is difficult to adjust and maintain. Plants that require a pH much different from that normally found in your garden are best

An alternative to soil that is gaining popularity amongst pond gardeners is the use of pea gravel or kitty litter as a planting medium. It is easy to use and doesn't contaminate the water. Submerged, emergent, marginal and bog plants can all be grown this way with the addition of fertilizer tabs at planting time according to package directions.

grown in containers or together in beds so you do not have to amend too large an area.

Water pH tends to influence the bacterial and fish populations more than it does the plants. Additives to adjust water pH are available at pond supply stores.

Potting and Planting

The potting or planting method used for each type of aquatic plant can vary slightly, but a few general guidelines apply to all water garden plants. To avoid dividing your container plants more often than necessary, choose container sizes that are large enough to hold the plants at maturity. (For plants that grow very large, compromise by using the largest containers that you can handle that fit comfortably into your pond.) Plants that need additional nutrition can benefit from slow-release aquatic fertilizer tablets placed in the pots before you add the soil and plants. Use thoroughly damp (but not muddy) soil to reduce both the air bubbling out of

Cabomba, a submerged oxygenator

the soil and excessive settling when the plant is lowered into the pond (or, with direct planting, when the pond is filled with water). To help prevent the soil, whether in a pot or directly in the pond, from getting mixed into the water and to stop fish from uprooting your plants as they search for food, top the soil with gravel or small rocks.

Submerged oxygenating plants often just need to anchor themselves and they will absorb the nutrients they require from the water. You can simply tuck them into the gravel at the bottom of the pond, or if your

Floating aquatic salvinia ferns spread quickly over the water's surface.

pond bottom is not lined with gravel, you can pot these oxygenators into pots of either gravel or soil.

Other submerged plants (with or without floating leaves), **emergent** plants and **marginal** plants all have similar potting or planting needs. Put them into a loamy pond mix topped with gravel or small, round rocks. The nature of their roots, whether fibrous or tuberous, determines the best way to situate them in the pot or underwater bed.

A fibrous-rooted plant generally forms a clump and should be placed in the centre of its container or planting area. The tuber of a tuberous-rooted plant usually has a cut end (where it was separated from a parent plant) and a growing end. Place the cut end against the edge of the pot or planting area to allow the growing end to expand into the available space. In both these situations you are allowing your plants to make the best use of the space before you have to divide them.

Floating plants can, of course, simply be scattered onto the pond's surface. Floating plants that like still water should be placed near the edge of the pond but away from the skimmer intake, water return and any stream or waterfall. Exposed rocks, bridges and plants that are anchored to the bottom help keep your floating plants in place.

Bog plants can be planted in a specially created bog garden, as described earlier in the book, or in wet areas bordering the pond. Be sure to maintain the soil at an adequate moisture level for their needs.

Pondside plants—annuals, perennials, trees and shrubs—are treated like regular garden plants. Compost makes a good addition to the soil, but avoid adding fertilizers that could leach into your pond during heavy rain and lead to excessive algae growth. If you are new to gardening or unfamiliar with any of these plants, consult a general gardening book or ask at your local garden centre for more information.

Maintenance

Regular maintenance of your pond and plants will keep your water feature looking its best and can reduce or prevent some problems from occurring. Pruning, removing dead material and checking for pest problems are just a few of the tasks that, when performed on a regular basis, can keep bigger jobs and problems at bay. Other tasks, such as hosing out your biological filter, should be done very infrequently because more frequent intervention can cause the very problems you are trying to avoid, in this case by reducing the bacterial population that is doing the filtering.

One thing that many pond plants, regardless of category, have in common is vigorous growth. In a small home pond, this vigorous growth can quickly fill your pond and throw your ecosystem out of balance. A certain amount of trimming and pruning may be required to keep the growth from swamping your pond. Regular trimming will also reduce the amount of material decomposing in your pond. Decomposing material produces gases that can be harmful to fish, some beneficial bacteria and some of the important insects and amphibians in your pond.

Fish often nibble on **submerged** plants, particularly the oxygenators, but not always enough to keep their persistent growth under control. Use a pair of scissors to trim their growth back regularly. A good trim in mid- to late summer may be sufficient to keep your submerged oxygenators looking tidy.

Floating plants and plants with floating leaves also warrant keeping an eye on. They should be allowed to cover no more than 60% of the water's surface. Open water allows the gases created by decomposition to escape easily and it lets in sunlight to feed your submerged plants. Floating plants that are spreading too widely can be scooped out and added to the compost bin. Trim back dead, damaged and older leaves of floating plants to prevent them from spreading too widely and stacking up on top of one another. Spent

Biological filters should not be cleaned with chlorinated water, such as city tap water, because the chlorine will kill the bacteria. It can take most of the summer to re-establish the bacteria population needed to keep your pond clear.

flowers can also be removed; this often encourages more flowering.

Marginal and **emergent** plants require a bit less ongoing maintenance over the summer. Flowering plants may benefit from deadheading—removing spent flowers—unless you want them to go to seed. Remove dead and dying foliage to reduce the quantity of plant material that accumulates and decomposes in your pond.

Pondside and **bog** plants are treated like trees, shrubs, perennials or annuals in other parts of the garden. Their maintenance requirements are fairly simple. Remove spent flowers as needed. Remove dead, damaged or diseased growth to keep plants looking neat and attractive. One task that is sometimes overlooked is watering. Because we build our ponds so that they won't leak water, pondside plants that like moist soil may need

A newly installed or freshly cleaned out pond will commonly reward your efforts with a vigorous bloom of algae. Things will start to equalize as the bacteria repopulate and the plants start to flourish and outcompete the algae.

supplemental watering. Bog gardens should also be checked regularly to make sure they are sufficiently moist.

You will have the most work in your pond in spring and fall. Spring is the time to give your pond a good clean-out, and fall is the time to get it ready for winter.

Spring Cleaning

A thorough clean-out in spring gets your pond ready for the year. This involves removing your fish and looking after any eggs or tadpoles of frogs and other amphibians, pumping or bailing out the water, scooping or pumping out any accumulated debris, hosing the rocks off a bit, cleaning the filters, replacing worn filter parts and adding fresh water. Not all ponds will need this level of cleaning annually, but a spring cleaning gives you a great opportunity to give your plants a little tender loving care.

If you do your clean-out in mid- to late spring, as the plants begin to sprout in the pond, you will have a good idea of what is alive and what is not. Clear any dead plants out of the pond. If you aren't sure if a plant is dead, you can always trim back any growth you think is dead and make a note to check back in a few weeks, when the water has warmed a little more.

Whether you clean your pond out in spring or not, you can push slow-release fertilizer tabs into the soil around your aquatic plants, particularly around heavy feeders such as water lilies and lotus plants, according to the package directions. Also in spring, you can work compost into

Removing whole spent flowering stem

Pinching off spent bloom or deadheading

the soil around the bases of your pondside plants to improve the soil without worrying about excess nutrients washing into the pond, which often happens with chemical fertilizers.

Marginal and pondside plants, in particular, may have been left to wither around the edges of your pond over winter without being cut back. Perhaps they were left to display decorative seedheads, to provide shelter for wildlife or to reduce the amount of wind your pond was exposed to during cold weather. Last year's growth should be cut back as or before the new growth emerges. Grasses and grass-like plants often produce dense tufts of growth that can be difficult to cut back once the new growth emerges.

As with the perennials in the rest of your garden, your water garden plants probably need dividing when they outgrow their space, begin to thin in the centre of the clump, flower less or seem to be growing less vigorously. Many will need fairly frequent division because they grow vigorously and can quickly outgrow containers or growing spaces.

Many plants recover quickly when they are divided in spring, just as they prepare to begin active growth, and plants that are grown directly in the pond are easiest to work with when the water has been removed. The rocks and gravel that cover the planting areas can be removed and the plants removed and divided if needed. Container-grown plants, too, can be examined to see if they have filled their containers.

Dividing perennial water garden plants isn't difficult and just requires a little knowledge about how each plant grows. Extra pieces can be composted or potted and

If your pond will be allowed to freeze over the winter and you won't be running the pump, you should remove it in the fall at the same time you remove any fish. Clean the pump out, store it in a bucket of water and plug it in from time to time to prevent hard water deposits from accumulating.

given away to friends and neighbours with ponds.

Working out of the wind, in the shade or on an overcast day can be easier on your plants and reduces their chances of drying out. Begin by removing the plant from its growing space or container and hosing any dirt away from the roots.

Plants that form clumps and have **fibrous** root systems can be split into several smaller pieces by teasing the clump apart by hand. Very large clumps may need to be split with a pair of garden forks. Replant the pieces right away and never let the roots dry out.

Plants that have **tuberous** roots require a little more effort to divide. Begin by determining which are the growing ends and which are the old, spent ends. Old tuberous sections may feel empty or seem shriveled or they may no longer have any leaves or fresh shoots emerging from them. Once you cut away any of these old sections, you may find that the remaining growth has been divided into pieces suitable for replanting. If any of the remaining pieces are still larger than you want them, cut them into smaller pieces. Be sure that each piece has some leaves growing from it. Remove any damaged parts before repotting because they will probably rot anyway. Once again, try not to let the roots dry out, and repot the plants right away.

Some tropical water lilies cannot be divided because they have very slow-growing tubers that grow vertically rather than spreading horizontally. Any damage to the tuber is likely to kill the plant.

Fall Preparation and Overwintering

As the nights begin to get colder and the first frost is expected, you can do a few things to get your pond ready for winter. Most water plants will die back completely in fall; it is best to remove as much of the dead or dying vegetation as you can to avoid having it decompose in the water. Most tropical plants should be moved to winter storage before the first frost (check the individual accounts to see which plants should be left until after the first frost). Also, some marginal plants may need to be

moved to a deeper spot in the pond so they will be below the ice line.

Most plants that are hardy in your area will happily overwinter right in the pond, but a few techniques will help ensure that your plants survive the winter problem-free. In most of our gardens, ponds over 45 cm (18") deep will only partially freeze. Having some of the pond remain unfrozen gives plants (as well as fish, amphibians and any other pond dwellers) the best chance to survive winter.

Oxygenators should be cut right back in fall. Some oxygenators develop small buds along their stems that drop off and sink to the bottom of the pond. You may wish to collect some of these buds and overwinter them indoors in a layer of mud at the bottom of a bucket of water. They should be kept in a cold but frost-free location, at about 5° C (40° F), to ensure that they remain dormant until spring. Another option is to take cuttings or plants to overwinter in an indoor aquarium. Otherwise, you can simply remove and compost the plants and then buy new ones in spring.

Almost all **floating** plants, like some of the oxygenators, develop buds that can be overwintered in the pond or in a layer of mud at the bottom of a bucket of water kept in a cold but frost-free location, at about 5° C (40° F). These plants can also be overwintered in an aquarium, but they often need more light than is normally found indoors. An artificial light, such as a fluorescent light intended for plants, may be needed to keep floating plants—particularly tropical ones— happy indoors. If you have a bright window or an artificial light set up, you may want to try overwintering your floating plants. If you don't have the space or the inclination, you can purchase new floating plants in spring.

Hardy **submerged, marginal** and **emergent** plants can be overwintered in the pond. Cut back the leaves in fall as each plant begins to go dormant. Plants grown directly in the pond can be left in place, but plants in containers should be lowered to the deepest part of the pond after you have cut back the foliage.

Marginal plants can also be planted into a regular part of the

A Hole in the Ice

Keeping a hole open in the ice is good for your pond and especially for your fish, because it allows gases to escape that might otherwise accumulate to toxic levels. However, pounding a hole through the ice once the pond freezes over can create shock waves that may stress or kill your fish. Run the pump year-round (or as long as practical) or use a bubbler and, especially below −12° C (10° F), a floating de-icer or heater (typically 1000 watts or more) to keep a hole open, at least to −18° C (0° F). The extreme nighttime winter cold found in some parts of Canada may overwhelm these devices, however, or they may cost more to operate than you are prepared to spend. There are 100-watt heaters available, designed to keep a hole free in the ice without costing a fortune to operate. If you expect the surface to freeze over for more than a few days, your fish will probably be better off in an unheated indoor aquarium for winter.

garden that is bare of annuals or vegetables for winter. Move them back to the pond in time for your spring planting. This technique is easiest with potted plants—just plant them, pots and all.

Tender and **tropical** marginal and emergent plants should be brought indoors for the winter or they can be replaced in spring. To overwinter tender and tropical plants indoors, you will need a bright location. Keeping them in watertight hanging baskets for winter is one popular method. Check them frequently to be sure they don't dry out.

Tender and tropical submerged plants need to be kept in deeper water than you can manage with a hanging basket, and they will need to be overwintered in an aquarium. Artificial light may be required if you don't have a bright enough spot. Lanky, pale growth indicates a need for more light.

Plants that are frost sensitive must be brought indoors before the temperatures drop significantly, even before the first frost. Once nighttime temperatures begin to drop below 10° C (50° F), bring these plants indoors. They may not recover from lower temperatures if you wait too long before bringing them in.

Don't fertilize plants when they are indoors; they will probably not be growing vigorously enough to need the extra nutrients.

When moving any of your plants back outside in spring, be sure to acclimatize them to the brighter light. Move them to a shaded location and gradually expose them to brighter light each day for two weeks before returning them to the pond. Do not return tropical plants to the pond until the water stays at about 21° C (70° F).

Propagation

Many gardeners are content to purchase whatever plants are locally available, and they never feel the need to try unusual plants or to increase the number of varieties in their ponds. Other people are intrigued by plants that are available only from seed, or they want to start cuttings from a friend's plants or they simply enjoy the challenge and satisfaction of growing plants from next to nothing.

Division is an easier, quicker way than seeding or cuttings to get more water garden plants. Most perennials can be split into several pieces once they are large enough. This topic is discussed in the maintenance section because you will have to divide most of your water plants from time to time, even if you don't want more of them, just to keep the plants healthy and to control their spread. Most slow-growing plants, even if they take years to fill their containers or growing spaces, can be divided if you want more of them. Think about the size the plant was when you first got it or how big similar plants are at the garden centre. As long as your plant divisions are about that size, you can quite likely divide your plant.

Seeding is a good way to grow lots of plants, grow unusual plants or breed your own new varieties. The process can be slow, and it may be many years before your plants mature—some seeds even take

Pulling a clump apart

Cutting and dividing tuberous perennials

more than a year just to germinate. The process, however, is not much different for water garden plants than it is for other garden plants. The seeds are planted in a flat tray or in pots. The soil is kept very moist or, in some cases, under water and is covered by clear plastic to

Prepared seed tray

Soaking seeds speeds germination.

is recommended for marginal and pondside plants, whereas the heavier loamy pond mix you use to plant aquatic plants is suitable for starting seeds of submerged plants. As the seedlings grow, be sure to keep the soil moist for marginal and pondside plants and wet or slightly under water for submerged and emergent plants.

The first one or two leaves that sprout, the 'seed leaves,' generally look completely different from the 'true leaves,' which sprout next and look more like the mature leaves. Once the seedlings have two or three true leaves, the plant can be transplanted to individual pots and grown on a bit before being moved to the water garden. Be sure to acclimatize them gradually to the outdoors, beginning with a few hours in the shade, before moving them out permanently. Submerged and emergent plants will have to be raised to a higher level than normal in the pond and gradually lowered as they mature. If they are in water that is too deep for them, the small, young plants may not get enough light.

Because their needs are not as exacting as those of the deeper-water plants, the easiest plants to grow from seed are marginal and pondside plants. The seeds for these plants are often readily available for purchase because many of them are also grown in gardens without water features.

Before some seeds will sprout, they require pretreatment to mimic the conditions they would experience in the wild. For example, seeds from cold-climate plants will often

keep the humidity level high. However, a common soil-borne fungus can cause the young seedlings to rot, usually at soil level. This is called 'damping-off,' and it can be an especially big problem for water plant seeds because the typically high soil moisture and humidity levels encourage the growth of fungi. Minimize the likelihood of damping-off by removing the plastic cover as the seedlings sprout, so that air can circulate freely. In addition, a sterilized soil mix intended for starting seeds sprout only after they have had a period of cold weather. To break their dormancy, you can keep them in your refrigerator for several weeks. Other seeds will have to be soaked in water to mimic a period of floods or heavy rains. Seeds with very hard outer coats will have to be scratched, as would happen if they were eaten by a bird, to allow water to penetrate. One way to do so is to rub them between two sheets of medium- or fine-grit sandpaper. All of these adaptations are examples of how plants have evolved to give their seeds the best chance of sprouting at a place and time that will permit them to successfully mature.

Some water garden plants, such as water lilies, produce seeds that are encased in a jelly-like coating that allows them to float and disperse from each other and the parent plant. The coating gradually dissolves in water, causing the seeds to sink to the pond bottom, where, under suitable conditions, they can germinate. When growing the seeds of these submerged plants, you may need to keep them completely under water in order to get them to sprout.

Cuttings can be used to start many, but not all, water garden plants. This technique is often a good way to obtain new plants without having to disturb the entire parent plant by dividing it. Plants that send up individual leaves from the roots cannot generally be started from cuttings but are usually easy to propagate by division. Branching plants that produce many leaves along their stems can usually be propagated by cuttings. Other water gardeners may be willing to give you cuttings from their plants, which will allow you to expand the number of kinds of plants in your pond without spending a lot of money.

If you plan to root your cuttings indoors, remember that indoor light levels are much lower than outdoors, so you may need to use high-intensity plant lights. When the weather is warm enough, you can also propagate cuttings outdoors, using large containers of water or raised water beds.

Scarifying seeds with sandpaper

Preparing seeds for cold treatment

Removing lower leaves

Dipping in rooting hormone

Firming cutting into soil

Newly planted cuttings

Healthy roots

Submerged oxygenators are often very easy to propagate by cuttings because their roots are not needed for the plants to live, but just to anchor themselves in the pond. Snip 5–15 cm (2–6") lengths from the tips of the growing stems. Bunch several stems and tie them together firmly, without damaging the stems. If you weight the bundle to make it sink in the water (for example, with a non-lead fishing weight or something made of stainless steel, so it won't rust), the stems will simply keep growing and will eventually send down anchor roots into the gravel bottom of the container or pond.

Cuttings of **submerged** and **emergent** plants can be started in containers of soil mix appropriate for the mature plant, with 2.5–15 cm (1–6") of water covering them. **Marginal** and **pondside** plants can be started in containers of moist or wet soil, but they will not need to be submerged.

Each cutting to be grown in soil should have a leaf node—the point at which a leaf attaches to the stem—just above its base, and it should have at least four nodes in total. Remove the leaves from the lowest two nodes and tuck the stems into the soil. Young, tender growth will root most readily, but older growth may also grow successfully. Once you see new growth emerging, the plant has probably rooted. Give the stem a gentle tug, being careful not to pull too hard. If it doesn't pull easily from the soil, then it has rooted.

If you have started several plants in the same container, transplant them to separate containers and grow them a bit before moving them to the pond, using the same acclimatization process as for plants started from seed.

Cuttings are also a great way to produce tender plants for the next growing season without having to overwinter large plants that you may not have room for. Take cuttings in late summer and grow them indoors over winter. When the parent plants die in fall, they can simply be pulled out of the pond and put in the compost bin. Once the weather has warmed sufficiently the next year, you can acclimatize your cuttings and introduce them to the pond.

Some plants produce their own **plantlets** as a natural way of spreading. In many cases, the plants send out shoots, sometimes called 'runners,' and the plants that form at the end can be removed from the parent plant once they have some roots of their own. Plants that send out long roots or rhizomes underground, such as many grasses and mints, can form new plantlets in a similar way. Some water lilies will sprout small plants where a leaf meets the leaf stem. These small plants can also be removed once they sprout some roots, or they may eventually detach on their own and then can be collected. Plant these into a tray of mud with 2.5 cm (1") of water covering them, then gradually increase the depth of the water until the new plants are ready to be introduced to the pond.

Problems & Pests

WATER GARDENS SHARE many of the same pests, diseases and problems that can afflict the rest of your garden but, as always, healthy plants and ponds are less susceptible to problems. Frequent observation is the most effective way to keep track of what is going on in your pond. Encouraging beneficial insects, birds and other pest-devouring organisms goes a long way toward keeping pest populations under control.

For many years, pest control meant spraying or dusting with the objective of eliminating every insect in the garden—the good and the bad. A more moderate approach is being advocated today. The goal is now to simply limit problems to levels at which negligible damage is done. A few nibbled leaves or periodic algae blooms are nothing to get overly excited about.

A moderate approach is particularly important in the water garden. Chemicals should be used only as a last resort because, as a group, they do more harm than good. When you treat a problem in one aspect of the water garden, you may upset the balance of the rest of the system. Poisons meant to eliminate pests can contaminate the water and kill off the beneficial bacteria and insects that help keep your water clear and the pond healthy, leaving the water garden vulnerable to other or repeat attacks. In addition, these poisons may endanger the gardener and his or her family.

It is possible to keep an attractive water garden without resorting to chemical applications. A responsible, organic pest-management program has four levels of control. Cultural controls are the most important.

Physical controls should be attempted next, followed by biological controls. Chemical controls should be used only when the first three possibilities have been exhausted.

Cultural controls are the gardening techniques used in the day-to-day care of your garden. Most cultural controls are simple and straightforward. To prevent pest and disease problems, grow plants in the conditions they prefer, particularly with the appropriate light levels and soil moisture or at their preferred pond depth. Choose resistant varieties of plants that are not prone to problems. Space the plants out (and keep them trimmed or divided) so that they are not stressed by competing

for light, nutrients and space. Remove any plants from the water garden that are repeatedly decimated by the same pests every year. Remove and destroy diseased foliage. Prevent the spread of disease by keeping your gardening tools clean and by tidying up fallen leaves and dead plant matter when they begin to accumulate and at the end of the growing season.

Physical controls are often a good way to deal with problems that your cultural controls have not prevented. Properly applied, they can be quite effective with a wide range of pests, from insects to large mammals. An example of such a control is picking insects off plants by hand, which is not as daunting a solution as it

seems if you catch the problem when it is just beginning. Other physical controls include water sprays, traps, barriers, scarecrows, noisemakers and natural repellents that make a plant taste or smell bad to pests. Garden centres offer a wide array of such products, athough not all are suitable for the water garden because some of them can contaminate the water. When applied to plant diseases, physical controls usually necessitate removing the infected plant or parts of the plant in order to keep the problem from spreading. Diseased or heavily infested material is often best put in the trash for disposal or burned (be sure to respect any local regulations that restrict outdoor burning), but items such as chewed leaves that are damaged but do not carry insects can safely be composted.

Biological controls make use of populations of natural predators.

Animals such as birds, snakes, frogs, spiders, lady beetles and certain bacteria can help keep pest populations at a manageable level if you encourage them to take up permanent residence in your garden. Many birds are attracted to water gardens and will feed on a wide variety of insect pests, particularly if the pond has a shallow area where they can easily drink and bathe. Beneficial insects are probably already living in your garden, and you can encourage them to stay and multiply by planting appropriate food sources. For example, many beneficial insects eat nectar from flowers such as yarrow and daisies. The best known applications of bacteria are likely *Bacillus thuringiensis* var. *kurstaki* (Btk) against caterpillars and *Bacillus thuringiensis* var. *israliensis* against mosquitoes, but other bacteria are available to target different insect groups.

Chemical controls should rarely be necessary in a water garden but, if you believe you must use them, some 'organic' options are available at local garden centres. Organic sprays can be as dangerous as synthetic chemical ones, but they are made from natural sources and will eventually break down into harmless compounds rather than accumulate in the environment. The main drawback to using any chemicals is that they often kill the things you want as well as those you don't. For example, most insecticides will kill the beneficial insects you have been trying to attract to your garden and most herbicides will kill garden plants as well as weeds. When using chemicals, be sure to apply them in the recommended amounts (more is *not* better) and to use them to combat only the pests or problems listed on the package. Proper and early identification of problems is vital in finding a quick solution. Before using chemical controls on pond (or bog) plants, remove them from the pond area to avoid contaminating the water. Treat them in a separate container and rinse them well before returning them to the pond.

Caution should be taken when using more than one chemical treatment because they may not be compatible with one another. The wisest approach is to wait 48 hours between using different products.

The following general listing describes some of the problems you may encounter in your water garden. Many problems only affect pondside plants, while others only afflict plants in the pond.

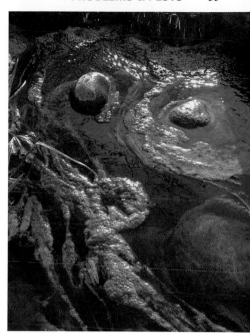

String algae may attach itself to some plants.

Algae

Several forms of algae exist. A soft, mossy growth that forms on rocks and other surfaces in the pond is beneficial, provides food for fish and other water dwellers and consumes excess nutrients. String algae (blanketweed), which forms stringy masses and clings to anything, can potentially smother plants and fish. Floating, single-cell algae will turn your pond an unattractive pea-soup green and block light to submerged plants.

What to Do: Avoid nutrient overload. Fertilizer runoff from surrounding lawns or flowerbeds, too many fish for the size of the pond, decomposing plant material and excess fish food all produce excess nutrients that are quickly consumed by algae. Plant enough oxygenators to outcompete the algae for nutrients—although green-water algae

Floating algae may turn your pond green.

peroxide as it decomposes. Bacterial additives that consume algae are available. Some insects, fish and other pond dwellers eat algae.

Animals

Ponds attract a wide variety of animals. Most are beneficial or neutral visitors that cause no problems, but a few can be destructive to the plants and fish that inhabit your pond. For example, raccoons can eat plants, overturn planting containers, dig up plants and even catch and eat your fish. Herons, eagles and other fish-eating birds can cause problems, and deer or rabbits may eat your plants.

What to Do: Make sure the fish have a place to hide. A length of PVC pipe can be laid at the bottom of the pond for fish to swim into when threatened, or you can make underwater caves using rocks, terracotta ware, etc. Most wading birds will land next to the pond and then walk in—running a string or wire

blooms are common in spring, they usually pass once oxygenator growth is more vigorous. Clumps of string algae can be removed by twirling a stick through the mass and lifting it out. Barley straw added to the filter or directly to the pond releases algae-destroying hydrogen

around the pond about 10–15 cm (4–6") above the ground will deter them. Put your plants in large containers well supported with rocks to make them more difficult to knock over. Fences can deter deer and rabbits. Motion-activated sprinklers can be used to startle animals when they approach the pond. Garden centres also offer natural deterrents containing substances such as predator urine or hot sauce, but these deterrents must be reapplied regularly.

Anthracnose

On pondside plants, this fungus can cause yellow or brown spots on the leaves along with sunken lesions and blisters on the stems, and it can even kill entire plants.

What to Do: Choose resistant varieties and cultivars. Keep the soil well drained, thin out the stems to improve air circulation and avoid handling wet foliage. Remove and destroy infected plant parts and clean up and destroy debris from infected plants when the growing season ends.

Aphids

These tiny, winged or wingless, pear-shaped insects are green, black, brown, red or grey. They cluster along the stems and on the buds and leaves of many plants, including water lilies. By sucking sap from the plants, they cause distorted or stunted growth, and their sticky 'honeydew' excretions encourage sooty mould growth. Woolly adelgids are a type of aphid.

What to Do: Squish or wipe off small colonies by hand or dislodge

Green aphids

them with a brisk water spray. Encourage predatory insects and birds that feed on aphids. You can spray serious infestations with insecticidal soap or neem oil according to product directions, but first remove the infected plants from the pond.

Beetles

Beetles come in many types and sizes, usually rounded in shape, with hard, shell-like outer wings covering membranous inner wings. Some are beneficial, e.g., ladybird beetles ('ladybugs'). Others, e.g., water lily beetles, Japanese beetles, blister beetles, leaf skeletonizers and weevils, eat plants. The wide range of chewing damage varies from small to large holes in or around leaf margins to the consumption of entire leaves or the areas between leaf veins ('skeletonizing') and can include flowers. Some beetles carry deadly plant diseases. For beetle larvae, see the entries under Borers and Grubs.

Beneficial predatory ladybird beetle larva

What to Do: Clear debris away from pond edges to eliminate over-wintering beetles. Pick beetles off at night and drop them into a container half-filled with soapy water (soap prevents them from floating and climbing out). Use a stream of water to knock the beetles into the pond, where fish can eat them.

Blight

Affecting mostly pondside plants, the many types of these fungal and bacterial diseases include leaf blight, fire blight, snow blight and tip blight. They cause leaves, stems and flowers to blacken, rot and die.

What to Do: Thin the stems to improve air circulation, keep mulch away from plant bases and remove debris from the garden when the growing season ends. Remove and destroy infected plant parts.

Borers

Varying in size, the worm-like larvae of some moths, wasps and beetles are very damaging plant pests. They burrow into stems, leaves and roots, destroying conductive (vascular) tissue, reducing structural strength and leaving tunnels that create sites for infection.

What to Do: Keep the plants as healthy as possible with proper fertilizing and watering. Remove the adults before they lay eggs. You may be able to squish the borers within the leaves. Remove and destroy infested plant parts and possibly entire plants.

Bugs (True Bugs)

These small insects, up to 13 mm (½") long, can be green, brown, black or brightly coloured and patterned. Many are beneficial, but a few pests, such as lace bugs, pierce plants to suck out the sap. They can inject toxins that deform plants, leave sunken areas where they pierced the plant, cause leaves to rip as they grow and cause buds and new growth to be deformed or dwarfed. The wounds these insects leave are also entry points for plant pathogens.

What to Do: Remove debris and weeds from around plants in fall to destroy overwintering sites. Remove the plants from the pond and spray them with insecticidal soap or neem oil according to product directions.

Canker

Most commonly found on pondside plants, many different bacterial and fungal diseases cause swollen or sunken lesions, often on the stems. Most canker-causing diseases enter through wounds.

What to Do: Maintain plant vigour and avoid causing wounds. Control borers and other tissue-dwelling pests. Prune out and destroy infected plant parts. Sterilize your pruning tools before and after use, such as with a 10% chlorine bleach solution (1 part bleach, 9 parts water).

Caterpillars

Bagworms, budworms, case bearers, cutworms, leaf rollers, leaf tiers, loopers and the like are the larvae of butterflies, moths and sawflies. They chew foliage and buds and sometimes completely defoliate plants.

What to Do: Removal from the plant is the best control—be careful not to damage the plant, use high-pressure water and soap or pick the caterpillars off small plants by hand. Remove the plants from the pond and spray them with the naturally occurring, commercially available soil bacterium *Bacillus thuringiensis* var. *kurstaki* (Btk), which breaks down the gut lining of caterpillars.

Clubroot

see Galls

Damping-Off

see p. 46 see p. 46

Fish

A welcome and necessary addition to the pond, fish can excessively consume, knock over or uproot plants.

What to Do: Grow small plants away from the fish—either divide them off with submerged netting or grow them in a separate container of water until they become established.

Use large, stable containers. A layer of small rocks or gravel on top of the planting soil can prevent fish from uprooting plants (the smallest rocks should be bigger than the mouth of your biggest fish). Feed your fish fruit and vegetables that they like.

Galls

These unusual swellings of leaves, buds, stems, flowers or fruit, typically caused by insects (such as *Hemerocallis* gall midge) or diseases, are often specific to a single genus or species of plant. Smut (treat as for Rust) can also cause galls.

What to Do: Cut the galls out of the plant and destroy them. Prevent galls caused by insects by controlling the adults before they lay eggs; otherwise, try to remove and destroy the affected tissues before the young insects emerge. Insect galls are generally more unsightly than damaging to the plant. Galls caused by diseases

Lygus bug

Leaf miner

watering) or even pull easily out of the ground.

What to Do: Any grubs found while digging can be tossed onto a stone path, driveway or patio for birds to devour or into the pond for the fish to eat. Apply parasitic nematodes or milky spore to infested soil (ask at your local garden centre).

Leaf Blotch
see Leaf Spot

Leafhoppers & Treehoppers
These small, wedge-shaped, green, brown, grey or multi-coloured insects (e.g., spittlebugs) jump around frantically when disturbed. They suck juice from the leaves, cause distorted growth and carry diseases such as aster yellows.

What to Do: Encourage predators by planting nectar-producing species such as yarrow. Wash the insects off with a strong spray of water or remove them from the pond and spray them with insecticidal soap or neem oil according to product directions.

Leaf Miners
These tiny, stubby larvae of some butterflies and moths may be yellow or green. They tunnel within a leaf, leaving winding, light-coloured trails. The results are unsightly rather than a major risk to the plant.

What to Do: Remove debris from the area in fall to destroy overwintering sites. Attract parasitic wasps with nectar plants such as yarrow. Remove and destroy infected foliage—you can sometimes squish the larvae by hand within the leaf.

often require destruction of the plant; avoid placing other plants susceptible to the same disease in that location, where it can lie dormant for many years.

Grey Mould (Botrytis blight)
Most likely on pondside or marginal plants, this fuzzy, grey fungus coats flowers or fruits, commonly in wet weather.

What to Do: Prevent disease by encouraging good air circulation and avoid handling wet plants. Remove and compost the infected plant material.

Grubs
Commonly found below soil level and usually curled in a 'C' shape, these larvae of various beetles have white or grey bodies and white, grey, brown or reddish heads. Problematic in lawns, they may feed on the roots of perennials, causing plants to wilt (despite regular

Leaf Spot

Small, brown or purple spots that grow to encompass entire leaves, which may drop, indicate a bacterium. Black, brown or yellow spots and withering leaves point to a fungus (e.g., scab, tar spot and leaf blotch).

What to Do: Avoid touching wet foliage or wetting the foliage when watering. Remove and destroy debris when the growing season ends. For fungal infection, remove and destroy infected plant parts. Bacterial infection is more severe and requires the removal and destruction of the entire plant. Sterilize the removal tools.

Mealybugs

Most likely on pondside plants, mealybugs are tiny, crawling insects related to aphids, that appear to be covered with white fuzz or flour. Their sucking damage stunts and stresses plants, and they excrete 'honeydew' that promotes the growth of sooty mould.

What to Do: Remove them by hand from small plants, wipe them off with alcohol-soaked swabs or wash the plants with soap and water. Remove and compost or destroy heavily infested leaves. Encourage or introduce natural predators such as mealybug destroyer beetle (their larvae look like very large mealybugs) and parasitic wasps (both are available at garden centres). Spray affected plants with insecticidal soap.

Midges

These tiny insects, which resemble mosquitoes, lay eggs in the water. The larvae hatch and look for water lily leaves. They burrow shallowly into the top of the leaf, leaving long, winding trails that rot through.

What to Do: Pick them off by hand or spray them off with the stream from a hose and allow the fish to eat them. Remove badly infested leaves and destroy them. Floating 'doughnuts' containing Bt can parasitize newly hatched larvae before they find the water lily leaves.

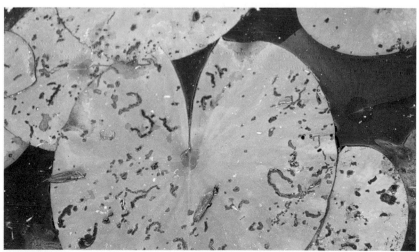

False leaf miner

Powdery mildew on leaves

Mildew

Yellow spots on the upper sides of leaves and downy, yellow, white or grey fuzz on the undersides indicates downy mildew. Powdery mildew is marked by a powdery, white or grey coating on leaf surfaces that doesn't brush off. Both are caused by fungi.

What to Do: Choose resistant cultivars. Space the plants well and thin the stems to encourage air circulation. Tidy any debris in fall. Remove and destroy infected leaves or other parts.

Mites

These tiny, red, yellow or green, eight-legged creatures are related to the spiders but do not eat insects. Almost invisible to the naked eye, they are usually seen moving on the undersides of plant leaves, and they may spin fine webbing on the leaves and stems. Examples include bud mites and spider mites. They suck the juice out of the leaves, which may become discoloured and speckled, turn brown and shrivel up.

What to Do: Wash the plants off daily with a strong spray of water until all signs of infestation are gone. Introduce predatory mites (available

from garden centres) or remove the plants from the pond and spray them with insecticidal soap.

Mould

see Grey Mould and Sooty Mould

Nematodes

Most likely in pondside plants, these tiny worms can affect either the foliage and stems or the roots. With foliar nematodes, the leaves develop yellow spots that turn brown, and then the leaves shrivel, beginning with the lowest leaves and working up the plant. Root-knot nematodes stunt a plant, may make it wilt, produce yellow spots on the leaves and cause tiny bumps or knots on the roots.

What to Do: Mulch the soil and add organic matter. Clean up debris in fall. Avoid touching the wet foliage of affected plants. Add parasitic nematodes to the soil. In extreme cases, remove and destroy the affected plants.

Rot

Several different fungi can rot different parts of the plant, possibly killing it. Crown rot (stem rot) affects the base of the plant, causing the stems to blacken and fall over and the leaves to yellow and wilt. Root rot destroys the roots, causing the leaves to yellow and the plant to wilt. White rot is a watery decay fungus that can affect any plant part— the cell walls appear to break down, releasing fluids.

What to Do: Keep the soil well drained and keep mulches away from the plant bases. Use care when digging around plants to avoid injuring them. Cutting the rot away may allow the plant to survive (less likely if it has submerged roots), unless the whole plant is affected.

Rust

Most likely on pondside plants, rust fungi cause pale spots on upper leaf surfaces and fuzzy or dusty, orange spots on the undersides. Examples are blister rust and hollyhock rust.

What to Do: Choose rust-resistant varieties and cultivars. Avoid handling wet leaves and provide your plants with good air circulation. Clear up garden debris when the growing season ends. Remove and destroy infected plant parts.

Scale Insects

Most likely on pondside plants, these tiny, shelled insects suck the sap, weakening and possibly killing the plants or making them vulnerable to other problems. Juvenile scale insects (crawlers) are mobile, but once a female scale insect pierces a plant with her mouthparts, she stays there for life.

What to Do: Wipe the adults off using alcohol-soaked swabs and spray with water to dislodge the crawlers. Prune off heavily infested branches. Encourage natural predators and parasites. Spray dormant oil in spring before the buds break.

Slugs & Snails

Slimy, smooth-skinned and grey, green, black, beige, yellow or spotted, these mollusks are snails if they have visible, spiral shells—otherwise, they are slugs. Slugs are restricted to land, but snails also inhabit the water. Possibly quite small but sometimes up to 20 cm (8") long, they can eat large, ragged holes in leaves or demolish entire seedlings. They leave silvery slime trails on and around plants. Often introduced by birds or with new plants, aquatic snails are common in ponds. Some, such as the ramshorn snail, are beneficial and eat algae. Others, such as the great pond snail, carry fish parasites and eat water plants.

Japanese beetles

What to Do: To capture unwanted snails in the pond, float a lettuce leaf on the water and scoop it out with a net after a day or two, along with the snails it has attracted. On land, tidy debris and remove hiding places. Attach strips of copper to wood around raised beds or to boards placed around susceptible groups of plants—slugs and snails will get shocked if they try to cross. Pick them off by hand in the evening or at night, especially during or after a rain, and squish them with your boot or drop them in a container of soapy water. Find and destroy egg masses. Set up traps. Spread wood ash or diatomaceous earth (available in garden centres) on the ground around the plants—it will pierce their soft bodies and dehydrate them. Slug baits containing iron phosphate are not harmful to humans or animals, and they control slugs very well when used according to product directions. If slugs or snails damaged the garden last season, begin controls as soon as the new green shoots appear in spring.

Smut
This fungus may cause galls or streaking on the leaves.
  What to Do: Treat as for rust.

Sooty Mould
This fungus forms a thin, black film on leaf surfaces that reduces the amount of light available for the plant.
  What to Do: Using a little soap on a damp cloth or sponge, wipe the mould off the leaf surfaces. Control insects such as aphids, mealybugs, whiteflies and leafhoppers that excrete 'honeydew' that the mould can feed on.

Thrips
Difficult to see, these tiny, slender insects are yellow, black or brown, with narrow, fringed wings. They may be visible if you disturb them by blowing gently on an infested flower. By sucking the juice out of plant cells, particularly in buds and flowers, they cause mottled petals and leaves, dying buds and distorted and stunted growth.
  What to Do: Remove and destroy affected plant parts. Encourage native predatory insects with nectar plants such as yarrow. For severe infestations, spray the plants with insecticidal soap or neem oil according to product directions (remember to treat affected pond plants away from the pond).

Viruses

Viruses (e.g., aster yellows, mosaic virus and ringspot virus) can cause stunted growth or the leaves and flowers to be distorted, streaked or discoloured.

What to Do: Viral diseases in plants cannot be treated. Control insects that spread them, such as aphids, leafhoppers and whiteflies. Destroy the infected plants.

Weevils

see Beetles

Whiteflies

Most likely on pondside plants, these tiny, white, moth-like flying insects live on the undersides of leaves and flutter up into the air when the plant is disturbed. They suck the juice out of the leaves, causing yellowing and weakened growth. They also deposit sticky 'honeydew' on the leaves, encouraging sooty mould.

What to Do: Destroy any weeds inhabited by whiteflies. Attract native predatory beetles and parasitic wasps with nectar plants such as yarrow. Construct a sticky, flypaper-like trap by mounting a tin can on a stake, wrapping it with yellow paper and covering it with a clear plastic bag smeared with petroleum jelly—discard and replace the bag when it is covered in flies. Spray severe cases with insecticidal soap.

Wilt

Mostly found on pondside plants. If watering doesn't help wilted plants, one of two wilt fungi may be at fault. With *Fusarium* wilt, the plant wilts and the leaves turn yellow and die; the symptoms generally appear first on one part of the plant before spreading. With *Verticillium* wilt, the plant wilts, the leaves curl up at the edges, turn yellow and drop off; the plant may die. Also see Grubs, Nematodes and Rot.

What to Do: Maintain healthy soil. Choose resistant plant varieties and cultivars. Both wilt fungi are difficult to control. Clean up debris when the growing season ends. Destroy infected plants and, in especially severe and extensive cases, consider solarizing (sterilizing) the soil before replanting—contact your local garden centre for assistance—keeping in mind that all soil organism populations will need to be reestablished afterward.

About this Guide

THE WATER GARDEN PLANTS in this book are organized alphabetically by their most familiar common names. Additional common names and scientific names appear after the primary reference. This system enables those who are familiar only with the common name of a plant to find that plant easily in the book. The botanical name is always listed (in italics), and readers are strongly encouraged to learn these botanical names. Common names are sometimes shared by several different plants, and they can change from region to region. Only the true botanical name defines the specific plant, everywhere on the planet.

The illustrated **Plants at a Glance** section at the beginning of the book allows you to quickly familiarize yourself with the different plants, and it will help you find a plant if you're unsure of its name.

Clearly indicated at the beginning of each entry are the plant's height and spread ranges, habit and hardiness zone. At the back of the book, you will find a **Quick Reference Chart** that summarizes different features and requirements of the plants; you will find this chart handy when planning diversity in your water garden.

Each entry gives clear instructions for planting and growing the water garden plant, and recommends many of our favourite selections. Note: if height and spread ranges or hardiness zones are not given for a recommended plant, assume these values are the same as the ranges at the beginning of the entry. Check with your local garden centre when making your selection.

Pests or diseases commonly associated with a water garden plant, if any, are also listed for each entry. Consult the **Problems & Pests** section of the introduction for information on how to solve these problems.

The
Plants

Anacheris
Brazilian Waterweed, Elodea
Egeria

Habit: submerged oxygenating or floating perennial or annual
Height: 30–90 cm (12–36") **Spread:** indefinite **Hardiness:** zones 5–8

THIS IS ONE of the most commonly available submerged plants for your pond. It grows quickly, consuming excess nutrients in the water and providing shelter and forage for fish and snails.

Growing

Anacherises grow best in **full sun**. They require no soil and can be left to **float** freely in the pond, or they may be planted in **gravel** or **sand,** in water 30–90 cm (12–36") deep, to keep them more or less in one spot.

These plants can survive winter as long as they don't freeze. Cut them back in fall so they stay below the ice. If you anticipate your pond freezing completely, you can treat these plants like annuals and plan to buy new ones in spring, or you can take a few cuttings to grow indoors in an aquarium over winter.

Tips

Anacherises are usually planted in bunches at the bottom of the pond. They grow vigorously, using up the nutrients that would otherwise feed algae. To keep algae growth under control, plant 5–20 bunches per m^2 (1–2 bunches per 1–2 ft^2) of water surface area.

Egeria, Elodea, and *Lagarosiphon* are three very similar plants with similar uses in the water garden. It can be difficult to tell them apart, but don't worry too much about which one you are buying—they will all consume excess nutrients in the pond.

Recommended

E. densa forms clumps of long, trailing, leafy stems. It bears small, white flowers at the water's surface in summer.

Anacheris stems break easily, and the pieces quickly become new plants.

E. densa with other submerged plants

Problems & Pests

Although snails and fish may nibble on young shoots, anacherises are generally problem free. String algae tends to attach to anacheris. Removal of both may be necessary to combat the problem if it occurs.

Angelica

Angelica

Habit: bushy pondside perennial **Height:** 90 cm–2.4 m (3–8')
Spread: 90 cm–1.2 m (3–4') **Hardiness:** zones 4–8

THESE PLANTS ARE at home in moist soil next to your pond. With their large, divided leaves and unique flowerheads, they lend an exotic air to the water garden.

All parts of angelica have a licorice scent. The stems can be candied and used to decorate cakes. The species also has a long history of use in Chinese medicine.

A. archangelica (all photos)

Growing

Angelicas grow well in **full sun to partial shade,** preferring some afternoon shade. The soil should be **fertile** and **moist**.

Start freshly ripened seeds in a cold frame in fall or early spring. Plant out the seedlings when they are small. Angelicas develop long taproots and resent being moved or divided.

These plants normally flower in their second year. Angelicas can live for several years, but they will die once they have flowered and set seed. Removing the flowerheads before the seed sets extends a plant's life. Angelicas left to set seed readily self-sow.

Tips

These large, exotic-looking plants add height to your waterside plantings and provide shade for smaller plants growing near them. Their adaptability to varied light levels makes them useful in both sunny and shady situations.

Recommended

A. archangelica (angelica, European angelica) spreads up to 1.2 m (4') and forms a mound of large, deeply cut foliage. Yellow-green flowers in large, rounded clusters appear atop tall, strong stems in early to mid-summer.

A. gigas (red-flowered angelica, Korean angelica) grows 1.5–1.8 m (5–6') tall and forms a large clump of deeply cut and lobed foliage. Tall, red stems bear clusters of purple flowers in mid- to late summer.

Problems & Pests

Occasional problems with powdery mildew, spider mites, aphids, leaf miners and leaf spot can occur.

Arrowhead

Sagittaria

Habit: marginal perennial or submerged oxygenator **Height:** 45–90 cm (18–36") **Spread:** 90 cm (36") or more **Hardiness:** zones 3–8

BEST KNOWN FOR their arrow-shaped leaves, these attractive shallow-water plants have a variety of leaf shapes. The summer flowers are produced over a long period, making these plants all the more desirable.

Growing

S. sagittifolia, *S. natans* and *S. latifolia* prefer **full sun** and tolerate partial shade. Plant them in **wet, gravelly soil**, either in submerged containers or directly in

S. sagittifolia *and*
S. latifolia *attract*
wildlife—the
tuberous roots are a
favourite snack of ducks
and other waterfowl.

the pond margins, in water 10–40 cm (4–16") deep, or up to 60 cm (24") deep for *S. natans*. *S. natans* can be slow to establish and may need protection from nibbling fish and snails until it becomes established.

Divide the plants in spring when they begin to outgrow their space.

Tips

S. latifolia and *S. sagittifolia* make attractive additions to the wet margins at the pond's edge. As vigorous spreaders, they are best suited to relatively large water features. Growing arrowhead in a container is a popular method of controlling its spread, but vigilance is still required to prevent shoots from escaping the pot over time.

S. natans is usually planted in bunches at the bottom of the pond. It grows vigorously once established, using up the nutrients that would otherwise feed algae. To keep algae growth under control, plant 5–20 bunches per m² (1–2 bunches for every 1–2 ft²) of water surface area.

Recommended

S. latifolia (duck potato) forms a large, tuberous clump and spreads up to 90 cm (36"). The base is underwater, and the arrow-shaped leaves emerge from the surface. It bears spikes of white flowers in summer.

S. natans (*S. subulata*, dwarf sagittaria) is a submerged oxygenator that forms a dense mat of bright green, grass-like leaves on the pond bottom. In shallow water, plants may develop floating leaves. It is hardy in zones 5–8, though it may survive in a colder climate at unfrozen depths in the pond.

S. latifolia (above & below)

S. sagittifolia (common arrowhead) forms a very large, tuberous clump that grows 90 cm (36") tall and can spread indefinitely. The arrow-shaped leaves emerge from the water, and the plant bears spikes of white flowers in summer.

Problems & Pests

Occasional problems with aphids, leaf spot, smut and spider mites can occur.

Astilbe

Astilbe

Habit: flowering pondside perennial **Height:** 25 cm–1.2 m (10"–4')
Spread: 20–90 cm (8–36") **Hardiness:** zones 3–8

THIS PERENNIAL GARDEN favourite adds a bright splash of colour to the pondside garden. The soft, plumy flowers and glossy foliage will thrive in moist, fertile soil, in a shaded spot next to your water feature.

With their fern-like foliage and showy, plumed flowers, astilbes are a favourite with both water gardeners and those without water features.

Growing

Astilbes grow best in **light to partial shade;** in full shade they do not flower as well. The soil should be **fertile, humus rich, acidic, moist** and **well drained**. Although astilbes appreciate moist soil, they don't like standing water.

Astilbes do self-seed, but the seedlings rarely resemble the parent plants. Pull them up if they will crowd out your more desirable plants. To maintain plant vigour, astilbes should be divided every three years or so.

A. x *arendsii* hybrids (above & below)

Tips

The colourful flower plumes and delicate foliage will brighten moist, shaded areas around your pond or alongside a woodland stream. Astilbes can be included in bog gardens, but they do best near the edges, where the soil is moist but not wet.

Recommended

A. x *arendsii* **hybrids** (astilbe, false spirea) grow 45 cm–1.2 m (18"–4') tall and spread 45–90 cm (18–36"). This large group of plants is commonly grown and available at many garden centres. Their lacy foliage comes in shades of green or bronze. The late-summer flowers bloom in a variety of shades of pink, peach or red and white or off-white.

A. chinensis (Chinese astilbe) is a dense, vigorous perennial that grows about 60 cm (2') tall and spreads about 45 cm (18"). It bears fluffy plumes of white, pink or purple flowers in late summer. **Var.** *pumila* is often more common than the general

species. It forms a low groundcover with dark pink flowers, about 25 cm (10") tall, with a spread of 20 cm (8").

Problems & Pests

Whiteflies, black vine weevils, Japanese beetles, powdery mildew, bacterial leaf spot and fungal leaf spot sometimes cause problems.

Bee Balm
Bergamot
Monarda

Habit: pondside perennial **Height:** 60 cm–1.2 m (2–4')
Spread: 30–60 cm (12–24") **Hardiness:** zones 3–8

BEE BALMS WILL keep your water garden humming with winged visitors. The flowers attract bees, hummingbirds, butterflies and other pollinators.

Growing

Bee balms grow well in **full sun to light shade**. The soil should be of **average fertility, humus rich, moist** and **well drained**.

These plants can be started from seed in spring, either indoors or outdoors in a cold frame. Divide your bee balms every two or three years to keep them vigorous. To encourage good air circulation, thin the new growth a bit as it sprouts in spring.

Tips

Use bee balms around the edges of your pond or include them at the edges of a bog garden where the soil is moist but not soggy.

Recommended

M. didyma is a bushy, mounding plant that forms a thick clump of stems with flowers in varied shades of red and pink. Powdery mildew is less of a problem on plants that have access to water, and mildew-resistant cultivars such as **'Gardenview Scarlet'** and **'Marshall's Delight'** are available.

Problems & Pests

Powdery mildew is considered the worst problem, but rust, leaf spot and leafhoppers can also cause trouble.

Fresh or dried bee balm leaves may be used to make a refreshing, minty, citrus-scented tea.

M. *didyma* (above), 'Marshall's Delight' (below)

Beech Fern

Thelypteris

Habit: perennial pondside fern **Height:** 30–80 cm (12–32")
Spread: 40–100 cm (16–40") or more **Hardiness:** zones 4–8

THIS WELL-BEHAVED, bright green fern softens the edges of the
pond and blends into the surrounding landscape.

*The recommended species on the
following page rarely suffer from
any problems.*

Growing

Beech ferns grow well in **full shade, light shade** or **partial shade**. The soil should be of **average fertility, humus rich, slightly acidic** and **consistently moist**.

T. plaustris may need frequent dividing to control its vigorous spreading, but the slow-growing, slow-spreading *T. decursive-pinnata* needs less frequent division.

Tips

These ferns make attractive additions to a shaded pondside garden or bog garden. *T. palustrus* takes up a lot of space and should be grown near a fairly large pond. *T. decursive-pinnata* is not as aggressive and can be included near a smaller pond.

Recommended

T. decursive-pinnata (*Phegopteris decursive-pinnata*, Japanese beech fern, beech fern) spreads 40–60 cm (16–24"), forming a mass of light green fronds that may become chartreuse in especially sunny locations.

T. palustris (marsh fern) grows about 60 cm (2') tall and spreads at least 1 m (40"). It forms a creeping mass of rhizomes from which the deeply lobed fronds emerge. Fertile fronds only grow in good light.

Fern-lovers appreciate T. decursive-pinnata *for its noninvasive habit, an attribute not shared by many other ferns.*

T. palustris (this page)

Birch

Betula

Habit: pondside or streamside trees
Height: 15–27 m (50–90')
Spread: 7.5–18 m (25–60')
Hardiness: zones 2–8

THESE LARGE TREES are admired for their foliage and interesting bark. They give a natural appearance to a water feature, creating light shade and ideal conditions for many pondside plants.

Growing

Birches grow well in **full sun to light shade**. The soil should be of **average to rich fertility, moist** and **somewhat well drained**. The species, described below, don't tolerate extended periods in waterlogged soil.

Minimal pruning is required. Remove dead, damaged, diseased or awkwardly growing branches as needed, but late summer and fall are the best times to prune. Sap tends to bleed excessively when cuts are made in spring.

Tips

By no means small trees, birches are often found growing naturally in damp areas, such as near streams, rivers, ponds and lakes. They will give your home water feature a natural appearance. Because birches generally cast only a light shade, many pondside plants thrive beneath them.

To give the appearance of several trees where there is room for only one, choose specimens with multiple trunks.

B. papyrifera (above & below)

Recommended

B. alleghaniensis (*B. lutea*, yellow birch) grows 18–24 m (60–80') tall, with a spread of 9–18 m (30–60'). The very flaky bark is golden brown, and the foliage turns bright yellow in fall. The young stems smell of wintergreen when broken. (Zones 3–7)

B. nigra (river birch, black birch, red birch) grows 18–27 m (60–90') tall and spreads 12–18 m (40–60'). It has shaggy, cinnamon brown bark that flakes off in sheets when it is young but thickens and becomes ridged as the tree matures. (Zones 4–8)

B. papyrifera (paper birch, canoe birch) grows 15–21 m (50–70') tall and spreads 7.5–14 m (25–45'). The white bark peels off in thin layers. In fall, the foliage turns varied shades of yellow and gold. (Zones 2–7)

The bark of B. papyrifera *has been used to make canoes, shelters, utensils and—as both the scientific and common names imply—paper.*

Problems & Pests

Birches can be afflicted by aphids, birch leaf skeletonizers, leaf miners, tent caterpillars and bronze birch borers. The borers usually attack stressed trees and can be fatal, but the birch species listed above are resistant to this pest if properly planted and cared for.

Bladderwort

Utricularia

Habit: floating perennial **Height:** 15 cm (6") in flower **Spread:** indefinite
Hardiness: zones 1–8

AS IS OFTEN the case with carnivorous plants, bladderworts make a rather unique addition to a pond. The flowering stems are often supported by a whorl of floating, bladder-like leaves, which are as decorative as the flowers.

Bladderworts can become invasive. Check with your local authorities—if any of these species are becoming a problem in your area, you may prefer not to use them in your water garden.

V. vulgaris (above), underwater stem and bladder (below)

Growing

Bladderworts grow best in **full sun** and a **slightly acidic** environment. Most **float** just below the water's surface, but some form a floating rosette of bladder-like leaves.

These plants form winter buds, which sink to the bottom of the pond in fall and produce new growth in spring. Bladderworts can form a large mass, usually near pond edges, and you may need to thin them out from time to time.

Tips

The small bladders that grow with the leaves suck in and consume tiny insects, such as mosquito larvae, and help to control their populations.

Recommended

U. inflata (inflated bladderwort) floats below the water's surface. The foliage is thread-like and lacy, with small bladders dotted throughout. A rosette of fleshy, floating leaves forms on the surface in early summer to support the flower stems and their bright yellow flowers. (Zones 5–8)

U. purpurea (purple bladderwort) is a floating plant with stems of thread-like, lacy foliage just below the surface. Pale pink, pale purple or white flowers grow several to a stem, and they emerge from the water in late summer. (Zones 3–8)

U. vulgaris (common bladderwort) is similar in appearance to *U. purpurea* but it produces stems of bright yellow flowers all summer. (Zones 1–8)

Problems & Pests

Bladderworts rarely suffer from any problems, but fish may nibble on the thread-like foliage.

Bleeding Heart
Dicentra

Habit: pondside perennial **Height:** 30 cm–1.2 m (12"–4')
Spread: 30–90 cm (12–36") **Hardiness:** zones 3–8

THIS BEAUTIFUL PERENNIAL, with its arching habit and delicate flowers, makes a lovely addition to the pondside garden, where fairly moist soil will keep it blooming for most of the summer.

Bleeding hearts are the perfect addition to a moist woodland garden. Plant them next to a shaded part of your pond or stream.

Growing

Bleeding hearts prefer **light shade** and tolerate partial to full shade. The soil should be **humus rich** and **evenly moist** but not waterlogged. Dry, hot summer weather can cause these plants to die back, especially with too much sun or dry soil. They will revive in fall with the return of cooler weather.

The fringed and common forms rarely need dividing, but the western species can be divided every three years or so.

Bleeding hearts may self-seed, and the new plants can be transplanted if desired.

Tips

With their fern-like leaves and dangling flowers, these delicate plants look wonderful next to a pond, where they soften the appearance of edging rocks. An arching habit that mimics the flow of the water makes them look good near a waterfall.

Recommended

D. eximia (fringed bleeding heart) grows 30–60 cm (12–24") tall and spreads about 45 cm (18"). It forms a loose, mounded clump of lacy, fern-like foliage and bears pink or white flowers, mostly in spring and sporadically over summer.

D. formosa (western bleeding heart) grows about 45 cm (18") tall, with a spread of 60–90 cm (24–36"). This low-growing, wide-spreading plant's pink flowers fade to white as they mature. The main flush of flowers occurs in spring, but they continue to bloom for most of summer. This

D. eximia (above), D. spectabilis (below)

bleeding heart is the one least likely to go dormant in summer.

D. spectabilis (common bleeding heart) forms a large, elegant mound 60 cm–1.2 m (2–4') tall, with a spread of 45–60 cm (18–24"). It blooms in late spring and early summer. The outer petals are pink and the inner ones are white.

Problems & Pests

Slugs, downy mildew, *Verticillium* wilt, viruses, rust and fungal leaf spot cause occasional problems.

Bog Bean
Buckbean
Menyanthes

Habit: marginal aquatic perennial **Height:** 10–30 cm (4–12")
Spread: indefinite **Hardiness:** zones 5–8

THESE PLANTS CREATE bold contrasts in the pond; their dark red stems, dark pink buds and white, delicately fringed flowers all stand out against the bright green leaves.

New roots often form at a bog bean's leaf nodes. These rooted sections can be removed to start new plants.

Growing

Bog beans prefer **full sun,** but they tolerate partial shade with reduced flowering. The soil should be **fertile, peaty** and **wet,** in up to 23 cm (9") of water.

Divide your bog beans as needed in spring or fall when they have outgrown their containers or to control their spread.

In places where bog beans are not hardy, they can be overwintered in a cool location indoors.

Tips

Bog beans can be grown in the marginal area around your pond or on the first shelf of your pond. The stems are often red, creating a striking contrast with the bright green leaves.

These plants are ambitious spreaders and may spread horizontally to invade the containers of other plants in the pond.

Bog bean is native to peat bogs and prefers acidic soil. If plants fail to thrive, they may need supplemental acid added to their soil.

Bog bean may take a few years to establish. Growth usually takes off in the third year once a strong root system has developed.

Recommended

M. trifoliata is a spreading plant with leaves that generally stand above the water. Small spikes of white flowers open from dark pink buds in early summer.

Problems & Pests

Rare problems with leaf gall can occur.

M. trifoliata (this page), with *Eichornia* & *Pistia* (below)

Brass Buttons

Cotula

Habit: marginal, bog- or pondside annual or short-lived perennial
Height: 15 cm (6") **Spread:** 30 cm (12") **Hardiness:** zones 6–8; treated as a
semi-hardy annual in colder zones

BRIGHT YELLOW FLOWERS are always a welcome addition to the
garden. These water-lovers, with their sunny dispositions, will
brighten up your pond.

Brass buttons rarely suffer from
any problems. Native to South
Africa, they tolerate hot weather
better than many other water
garden plants.

C. coronopifolia (photos this page)

Growing

Brass buttons prefers **full sun** with **average, humus-rich, moist to wet soil,** and water up to 5 cm (2") deep.

Direct sow the seeds in spring. Where the plants are hardy, divide them in fall every year or two to encourage plant vigour. Deadheading prolongs flowering.

Tips

Brass buttons can be used in bog gardens, in pondside plantings or between the rocks at the pond's edge.

Brass buttons is one of the few annual water garden plants. It grows and flowers quickly in the first year. As with many members of the aster family, brass buttons' seeds are easy to collect so you can have plants again the following summer. Deadheading will prolong flowering, but when the flowering slows, you should allow the plants to go to seed. Collect the flowerheads once they dry and before they shed their seeds. Store the seeds in a cool, dry location for the

winter and start them in early spring so the plants will be ready for transplanting once the pond warms up.

Recommended

C. coronopifolia forms a low, spreading mound that produces bright yellow flowers in summer.

Though the flowers are considered the main attraction, the bright green foliage is also very decorative.

Buckler Fern
Wood Fern, Shield Fern
Dryopteris

Habit: pondside or marginal perennial fern **Height:** 12"–4' (30 cm–1.2 m)
Spread: 12–40" (30–100 cm) **Hardiness:** zones 2–8

THIS LARGE GROUP of ferns has variable fronds and habits. In general, buckler ferns grow in individual clumps that spread to form a mass of plants, useful for covering a medium to large area.

Buckler fern and its close relatives are among the easiest ferns to grow.

D. filix-mas (above)

Growing

Buckler ferns grow best in **partial shade**. The soil should be **humus rich** and **moist to wet**.

Divide these ferns in spring or fall if you wish to control their spread or to propagate them.

Tips

Include these large, impressive ferns in a shaded area next to your pond, or use them in a bog garden or in the overflow area of your water feature.

Recommended

D. carthusiana (toothed wood fern) grows 60–90 cm (24–36") tall and spreads about 30 cm (12"). This creeping fern forms a small clump.

D. dilatata (*D. austriaca*, broad buckler fern) grows 30–90 cm (12–36") tall and spreads 60–90 cm (24–36"). It forms a small clump, with all the fronds emerging from the centre.

Cultivars with frond variations are available. (Zones 4–8)

D. filix-mas (male fern) grows 75 cm– 1.2 m (30"–4') tall and spreads 60–100 cm (24–40"), forming a clump of lacy fronds. Cultivars with frond variations are available.

Problems & Pests

Occasional problems with leaf gall, fungal leaf spot and rust may arise.

Bugbane
Snakeroot
Cimicifuga

Habit: pondside perennial **Height:** 90 cm–2.1 m (3–7') **Spread:** 60 cm (2')
Hardiness: zones 3–8

THESE PLANTS FORM a neat mound of foliage, but the flowers, produced on long spikes, give the plants a more erratic and unusual appearance.

Growing

Bugbanes grow best in **partial to light shade**. The soil should be **fertile, humus rich** and **moist**. Bugbanes do not like competing with other plants and don't do well when planted between the roots of trees or vigorous shrubs. Unless given a bit of support—a peony hoop works well—these plants may flop over.

Because these plants resent being disturbed, division is not recommended. Small sections of the rhizomes can be carefully removed to propagate more plants, though.

Tips

Bugbanes are attractive when mass-planted in the moist edges of a large pond. They appreciate the shade of a tree, but be sure to plant them far enough away so that their roots are not in direct competition with it.

Because their flower scent is often unpleasant, bugbanes are usually best relegated to the far side of the pond, where you can enjoy the sight without the smell. For close-up enjoyment, choose sweet-scented cultivars.

Recommended

C. racemosa is a large, clump-forming perennial. Tall spikes of unpleasantly scented, white or off-white flowers are produced in late summer. Purple-leaved cultivars are available, and **'Brunette'** also has sweet-scented, light pink flowers.

Bugbanes are native to eastern North America and rarely suffer from any problems.

C. racemosa 'Brunette' (above), *C. racemosa* (below)

Bugleweed

Ajuga

Habit: pondside perennial groundcover **Height:** 15–30 cm (6–12") **Spread:** 45–60 cm (18–24") **Hardiness:** zones 2–8

THIS PLANT IS a favourite in the perennial garden; its ability to grow between rocks and stepping stones makes it an ideal cross over to the pond garden.

Although some kinds of bugleweed spread aggressively, many cultivars are far more civilized and less likely to become invasive.

Growing

Bugleweeds grow well in **light to partial shade** and tolerate full shade. In full sun, the foliage is prone to scorching. These plants adapt to most soil types and conditions, but they grow best in a **moist**, but not water-logged soil. Winter mulch is recommended if snow cover isn't dependable in your garden and if your winter temperatures regularly drop below −18° C (0° F).

Divide these plants during the growing season, whenever they appear to be thinning out in the middle.

Tips

Bugleweeds make excellent ground-covers beneath shrubs, trees and other perennials around the edges of your water garden. Their dense growth suppresses most weeds.

A spreading and trailing habit makes them well suited to a spot next to a waterfall, where they may even trail into the water. In fall, remove any growth trailing in the water to prevent rotting material from accumulating in your pond.

Because most bugleweeds with interesting foliage do not come true to type from seed, many gardeners remove any new growth or seedlings that don't show the hybrid leaf colouring.

Recommended

A. genevensis (Geneva bugleweed) is a noninvasive, upright species that spreads 45 cm (18"). It bears blue, white or pink flowers in spring.

A. reptans (common bugleweed) is a low, quick-spreading groundcover that grows about 15 cm (6") tall.

A. reptans 'Catlin's Giant' (opposite), 'Pat's Selection (above)

Short spikes of blue flowers are produced in spring. Many cultivars have been developed for their variable, attractive foliage that grows in solid or variegated shades of red, purple, bronze, green and cream. (Zones 3–8)

Problems & Pests

Occasional problems with crown rot, leaf spot and root rot can be avoided by providing good air circulation and ensuring that the plants are not standing in water for extended periods.

A. reptans 'Chocolate Chip' (below)

Cabomba
Fanwort
Cabomba

Habit: submerged oxygenating perennial or annual **Height:** 20–40 cm (8–16")
Spread: indefinite **Hardiness:** zones 5–8

THESE BEAUTIFUL, PLUMY plants soften the appearance of the
pond while consuming excess nutrients from the water and providing
food and habitat for small fish.

Growing

Cabombas grow well in **full sun to partial shade**. They dislike moving water and should be planted in **still water** 20–50 cm (8–20") deep. Soil is not necessary, but they can be planted in coarse **sand** or **gravel** to hold them in place.

Cut your cabombas back in fall to below the usual ice depth. If you expect your entire pond to freeze over winter, you can take cuttings in late summer and grow them in an indoor aquarium. Otherwise, purchase new plants each spring.

Tips

Cabombas consume excess nutrients and add oxygen to the water. To reduce algae growth, plant 5–20 bunches per m² (1–2 bunches for every 1–2 ft²) of water surface area.

Recommended

C. caroliniana forms a clump of long stems with feathery foliage. Slender stems bearing white or pink flowers emerge from the water in summer.

C. aquatica forms a clump of long stems with fine, feathery foliage. Yellow flowers bloom above the water's surface on long, narrow stems. This species is most often sold in aquarium shops and it is not winter hardy in Canadian ponds.

Popular aquarium plants, cabombas can be purchased at pet shops that carry aquarium supplies, and they rarely suffer from any problems.

C. caroliniana (above & below)

Calla Lily

Zantedeschia

Habit: marginal aquatic or pondside perennial **Height:** 40–90 cm (16–36")
Spread: 20–60 cm (8–24") **Hardiness:** zone 8 or tender perennial

A BEAUTIFUL ARRANGEMENT of creamy white calla lilies makes
these plants worth overwintering in areas where they aren't hardy.

*Although they
grow quite large,
calla lilies can be
grown as houseplants
year-round, but they
benefit from spending
summer outdoors,
whether you have a
pond or not.*

Growing

Calla lilies grow best in **full sun**. The soil should be **fertile, humus rich** and **moist to wet**. They can be planted in water up to 10 cm (4") deep, or 30 cm (12") for *Z. aethiopica*. Growing callas in containers makes it easier to bring them indoors for winter. Reduce watering in winter, keeping the soil just moist.

Divide the plants as needed in spring when they begin to outgrow their containers or to propagate new plants.

Tips

These beautiful and exotic plants will give your water feature a tropical flavour.

Rather than moving large, cumbersome plants, it is sometimes easier to remove small divisions in fall for overwintering indoors.

Recommended

Z. aethiopica grows about 90 cm (36") tall and spreads about 60 cm (2'), forming a clump of arrow-shaped, glossy green leaves. It bears white flowers from late spring to mid-summer. Several cultivars are available. This species can survive winter on the West Coast if its container is completely submerged in the pond. (Zone 8)

Z. elliottiana (yellow calla, golden calla) grows 60–90 cm (24–36") tall and spreads 20–30 cm (8–12"), forming a basal clump of white-spotted, dark green, heart-shaped leaves. This species bears yellow flowers in summer and is a parent plant of many popular hybrids. (Grown as a tender perennial)

Z. aethiopica (above); *Z. rehmannii* (below)

Z. rehmannii (pink calla) grows about 40 cm (16") tall and spreads about 30 cm (12"), forming a basal clump of narrow, dark green leaves. This species bears pink, white or dark purple flowers in summer and is also a parent plant of many popular hybrids. (Grown as a tender perennial)

Problems & Pests

Rot, grey mould, rust and viral diseases can occur.

Canadian Hemlock
Eastern Hemlock
Tsuga

Habit: pondside evergreen tree **Height:** 12–24 m (40–80'); smaller cultivars are available **Spread:** 7.5–12 m (25–40'); smaller cultivars are available **Hardiness:** zones 3–8

DELICATE-LOOKING HEMLOCK, with its dark green needles, is one of the most beautiful native evergreens. It is often found growing naturally in low, moist areas alongside streams, rivers, ponds and lakes.

Several other species of Tsuga *exist, including two West Coast natives that grow too large for many gardens. The eastern hemlock has the most cultivars.*

Growing

Hemlocks grow well in any light from **full sun to full shade**. The soil should be **humus rich, acidic, moist** and **fairly well drained**. They grow best in cool, moist conditions and are sensitive to air pollution. Because they can suffer from salt damage, they may not do as well near salted walkways or driveways.

Pruning is rarely required, but it can be done to shape these trees, particularly if you begin when they are young.

T. canadensis 'Jeddeloh' (above), *T. canadensis* (below)

Tips

Attractive evergreens in a variety of forms beautify pondside plantings. The dwarf and low-growing hemlock cultivars are welcome additions because of their soft needles and compact habits. Weeping forms of hemlock can be planted near a waterfall to blend it more naturally into the surrounding landscape.

Recommended

T. canadensis is a graceful, narrowly pyramidal tree that grows 12–24 m (40–80') tall and spreads 7.5–12 m (25–40'). Native to eastern North America, it is often found growing in moist woodlands, and next to streams and other natural water features. Many cultivars are available, including dwarf, prostrate, weeping and yellow-needled forms.

Problems & Pests

Stress-free trees have few problems, but aphids, mites, scale insects, weevils, woolly adelgids, grey mould, needle blight, rust and snow blight can be problems when these trees are stressed.

Cattail

Typha

Habit: marginal aquatic perennial
Height: 60 cm–1.5 m (2–5') **Spread:** 30 cm (12")
to indefinite **Hardiness:** zones 2–8

THESE PLANTS ARE very
common in ditches and around
natural lakes and ponds in
Canada; no garden pond seems
complete without at least a
dwarf plant or two.

Growing

Cattails grow well in **full sun to partial shade**. The soil should be a **wet, loamy** pond mix, in water about 10–40 cm (4–16") deep. Cattails can be grown in containers or planted directly in the pond.

Divide the plants in spring to control their spread or when they have outgrown their containers.

Tips

Cattails can be grown on the shallowest pond shelf and at the edges of the pond. They can also be grown in moist, boggy areas next to the pond. Dwarf cattail is suitable for small ponds and even container ponds.

The flower spikes are popular choices for dried flower arrangements.

T. angustifolia (above), *T. minima* (below)

Recommended

T. angustifolia (narrow-leaved cattail) grows up to 5' (1.5 m) tall and can spread indefinitely, forming a dense clump of upright, narrow foliage. The dense, brown, 10–20 cm (4–8") flower spikes develop in midsummer and last until late fall.

T. minima (dwarf cattail) grows 60–80 cm (24–32") tall and spreads 30–40 cm (12–16"), forming a clump of upright, slender foliage. The flower spike is rounded in appearance and quite short, at just 2–5 cm (¾–2"). (Zones 3–8)

Problems & Pests

Rare problems with leaf spot can occur.

The larger common cattail, T. latifolia, *is too aggressive for most home water features.*

Cedar
Arborvitae
Thuja

Habit: pondside evergreen shrub or tree **Height:** 6–15 m (20–50'); smaller cultivars are available **Spread:** 3–6 m (10–20'); smaller cultivars are available **Hardiness:** zones 2–8

CEDAR IS A mainstay in many Canadian gardens. It lends itself wonderfully to pondside plantings, enjoys moist conditions and provides screening and colour year-round.

Named arborvitae *(Latin for 'tree of life') because the vitamin C in its foliage and bark saved Jacques Cartier's crew from scurvy, the white cedar was grown in Europe as early as 1536.*

Growing

Cedars prefer **full sun** but tolerate some shade. The soil should be of **average fertility, moist** and **fairly well drained**. Some **shelter** from winter winds helps prevent drying of the foliage, which can cause a drab brown appearance or even dead branches.

Cedars rarely need pruning and naturally maintain a tidy shape. Dead branches can be pruned out as needed in spring.

Tips

A soft appearance makes this moisture-loving evergreen an attractive choice for a spot near a water feature. It is particularly well suited to growing in small groups, and its quick growth can provide privacy and shelter for sitting areas.

If deer keep eating your *T. occidentalis* foliage, consider growing *T. plicata* instead—deer find it less appealing.

Recommended

T. occidentalis (white cedar, eastern arborvitae) can grow to about 18 m (60') tall and spread 10–20' (3–6 m) in much of its native eastern and central North America. In cultivation, it grows about half as tall or less. Dozens of available cultivars offer diverse features, such as yellow foliage, dwarf, rounded or upright habits and better winter colour retention. (Cultivars may be less cold hardy.)

T. plicata (western redcedar, western arborvitae) can grow up to 60 m (200') tall along its native Pacific Coast, but it rarely grows over 15 m

T. occidentalis 'Little Gem' (above)

(50') where it is hardy in the rest of Canada. This narrowly pyramidal evergreen grows quickly. The foliage stays bright green all winter. Smaller cultivars, generally 6 m (20') tall and spreading 3 m (10'), are available. (Zones 5–8)

Problems & Pests

Possible but infrequent problems include bagworm, heart rot, leaf miners, scale insects, blight, canker and red spider mites. To distinguish leaf miner damage from winter browning, hold the branch tips up to the light and look for tiny caterpillars feeding inside. Trim and destroy any infested foliage before June.

T. occidentalis 'Sherwood Moss' (below)

Chameleon Plant
Orange Peel Plant
Houttuynia

Habit: marginal or pondside perennial **Height:** 15–30 cm (6–12")
Spread: indefinite **Hardiness:** zones 4–8

H. CORDATA 'CHAMELEON' has brightly coloured stems and foliage that make this cultivar a popular addition to stream or pond edges, despite its rather vigorous nature.

Chameleon plants spread by rooting shoots as well as by rhizomes, and they may escape containers intended to control their growth. Keep your garden shears handy to trim plants back if they begin to threaten their neighbours.

H. cordata 'Chameleon' (above & below)

Growing

Chameleon plants grow well in **full sun to light shade**. The soil should be of **average fertility, humus rich** and **moist to wet**. They prefer to be above the waterline but will grow in up to 10 cm (4") of water. Plant them in containers and divide them in spring or fall to control their spread.

Tips

Chameleon plants make a beautiful groundcover for the edge of the pond. Next to a waterfall, they will scramble up or down the slope and over any rocks in the way.

Recommended

H. cordata is a spreading, scrambling plant. Crushing or brushing against the leaves releases a distinct citrus scent. What appear to be white summer flowers are actually tiny, dense spikes of flowers surrounded at the base by 4–6 bracts. The stunning cultivar **'Chameleon'** ('Tricolor'), which has red stems and leaves brightly variegated in shades of green, yellow, red and off-white, accounts for almost all garden plantings. It is also supposed to be less invasive, but most gardeners have not found it to be so.

Problems & Pests

Slugs and snails may consume the foliage.

Club Rush

Zebra Rush

Schoenoplectus (Scirpus)

Habit: evergreen marginal perennial **Height:** 90 cm–1.5 m (3–5')
Spread: 60 cm (2') or more **Hardiness:** zones 5–8

DENSE CLUMPS OF tall, narrow leaves emerge from the water in shades of chartreuse and green, sometimes with white bands. These plants sway with the wind or the movement of the water.

Club rushes, which are still often sold under their old genus name Scirpus, *rarely suffer any problems.*

'Zebrinus' (above & below)

Growing

Club rushes prefer **full sun**. The soil should be **fertile** and **moist to wet**, in water up to 40 cm (16") and preferably **still to slow moving,** not near a waterfall. Use containers or plant these rushes directly in the pond.

Divide the plants as needed in spring or fall when they have outgrown their containers or to control their spread. Zebra rush needs to be divided every two years to maintain its coloured banding and to prevent the stems from reverting to solid green.

Tips

Swaying and rustling gently in a breeze, these slender plants look attractive at the edges of a pond. Planted closer to the centre of the pond, they provide shade and shelter for fish and add an interesting vertical element to your water feature.

Recommended

S. lacustris is an upright, grass-like plant with inconspicuous flowers. **'Albascens'** has creamy white, vertical stripes on the leaves, which give the entire plant a yellow-green appearance. **Subsp**. *tabernaemontani* **'Zebrinus'** (zebra rush) has creamy white, horizontal bands on the leaves.

Columbine

Aquilegia

Habit: pondside perennial **Height:** 20–90 cm (8–36")
Spread: 30–45 cm (12–18") **Hardiness:** zones 2–8

THESE DELICATE NODDING flowers stand on thin stems above
mounds of lacy foliage, and add a colourful air to your pondside
plantings in early summer.

Growing

Columbines grow well in **partial shade**. The soil should be **fertile, moist** and
fairly well drained. They don't like standing water but will adapt to most
other soil conditions.

*Columbine's dainty, suspended flowers
attract butterflies, hummingbirds and
other pollinators.*

Columbines grow easily from seed. They hybridize and self-seed frequently. Although hybrid seedlings may not resemble their parent plants, they are likely to be interesting and attractive and so are worth keeping regardless.

Division is not required but can be done in spring to propagate desirable plants. Because columbines resent having their roots disturbed, the new plants can take a while to establish.

Tips

Columbine makes an attractive addition to the plantings that surround your water feature. It is a good choice for a rocky crevice, particularly in a shaded area where sun-loving rock plants have a difficult time growing.

Recommended

A. canadensis (wild columbine, Canada columbine) grows up to 60 cm (2') tall, spreads about 30 cm (12") and bears yellow flowers with red spurs. It is native to most of eastern North America.

A. **Hybrids** (hybrid columbines) generally form mounds of delicate foliage and may be dwarf, growing only 20 cm (8") tall, or large, growing up to 90 cm (36") tall. They have been developed mainly to produce showy flowers in a wider range of colours than is found in any single species. Shades of yellow, white, red, pink, purple or blue are available, with similar or contrasting spurs.

A. vulgaris (European columbine, common columbine) grows about 90 cm (36") tall and spreads 45 cm (18"). The flowers range from blue

A. Hybrids 'McKana Giant' (above)

and purple to red, pink and white. This species has been used to develop hybrids and cultivars with flowers in a variety of colours.

Problems & Pests

Leaf miners, mildew, rust, fungal leaf spot, aphids and caterpillars can trouble columbines. Damaged foliage, particularly foliage damaged by leaf miners, can be removed and destroyed; new foliage will fill in quickly.

A. canadensis (below)

Common Cotton Grass

Eriophorum

Habit: marginal aquatic perennial **Height:** 20–40 cm (8–16")
Spread: 60 cm (2') or more **Hardiness:** zones 4–7

THIS LOW-GROWING, GRASSY plant bears tufted, cottony flowers, making it a unique addition to moist soil or shallow water around the edges of your pond.

Neither children nor adults can resist touching the fuzzy flowers of cotton grass.

E. angustifolium (above & below)

Growing

Cotton grasses grow best in **full sun**. The soil should be **acidic** and **wet**, and **peat** can be added to your usual pond planting mix. If you plant in water, it should be no more than 5 cm (2") deep.

In areas with poor or inconsistent snow cover these plants should be mulched for winter.

Cotton grasses like plenty of room to spread. Divide them in spring when they have outgrown their containers or to control their spread.

Tips

Attractive additions to a bog garden, cotton grasses can also be planted in the margins of your pond or in moist areas around it.

If your cotton grass fails to thrive, the soil may not be acidic enough. The plants are native to peat bogs and may need to have their soil amended or fertilized with an acidic fertilizer.

These plants are native to northern regions of Europe, Siberia and North America, and they tend to grow best where the summer temperatures don't frequently exceed 30° C (86° F).

Recommended

E. angustifolium forms a tufted clump of narrow, grass-like leaves and produces fluffy, white flowers in spring or summer.

Problems & Pests

Rare problems with rust can occur.

Corydalis
Corydalis

Habit: pondside perennial **Height:** 30–45 cm (12–18")
Spread: 20–30 cm (8–12") or more **Hardiness:** zones 3–8

THESE CHARMING, LACY-LEAVED plants, with their yellow, blue or white flowers, fill spaces between rocks and around other plants beside the water garden.

Corydalises may die back in hot weather, but they usually produce fresh growth once the weather cools again in late summer and fall.

Growing

Corydalises prefer **light to partial shade** with morning sun. The soil should be of **average to rich fertility, humus rich** and **moist** but **fairly well drained**.

These plants are proving to be more hardy that they were previously thought. In gardens where snow cover is inconsistent and temperatures regularly drop below –18° C (0° F), mulch the plants for winter.

These plants self-seed, and the young seedlings can be transplanted to new locations. Although corydalises can be divided, doing so is not recommended because they resent having their roots disturbed and take a long time to reestablish.

Tips

Corydalises appreciate the cooling effect a pond has on the local environment. Tuck them between the rocks that surround your pond or plant them beneath the trees and shrubs that surround your water feature. The ferny foliage and light, airy habit look especially attractive near a waterfall.

Recommended

C. flexuosa (blue corydalis) is an erect plant that grows up to 30 cm (12") tall and spreads 20 cm (8") or more. It bears blue spring flowers. (Zones 4–8)

C. lutea (yellow corydalis) is a mound-forming perennial that spreads 30 cm (12") or more. It bears yellow flowers from late spring often to early fall. One of the hardiest species, it is also the most vigorous and can become invasive.

C. lutea (above & below)

C. ochroleuca (white corydalis) is similar in habit to *C. lutea* and grows about 30 cm (12") tall, with an equal spread. It bears white or off-white flowers in late spring and summer. (Zones 5–8)

Problems & Pests

Rare problems with downy mildew and rust are possible.

Curled Pondweed

Potamogeton

Habit: submerged oxygenating perennial   **Height:** up to 4 m (13')
Spread: indefinite   **Hardiness:** zones 6–8

THIS PLANT'S TRANSLUCENT green leaves and undulating leaf
edges make it stand out among the more common feathery underwater plants.

*Although their maximum size
may seem daunting, curled
pondweeds are among the
least aggressive of submerged
water plants, and they rarely
suffer from problems.*

Growing

Curled pondweeds grow well in **full sun to partial shade**. Add **sand** or **gravel** to your usual **loamy** pond soil mix and plant them **underwater**.

Cut the plants back as needed during the growing season to control their spread.

Curled pondweeds may survive winter outdoors if they are trimmed back to below the expected ice level before the pond freezes. Where these plants are not hardy, take cuttings in late fall and overwinter them indoors in an aquarium.

P. crispus (above & below)

Tips

These attractive plants consume excess nutrients and add oxygen to the water. To reduce algae growth, plant 5–20 bunches per m^2 (1–2 bunches for every 1–2 ft^2) of water surface area.

Though curled pondweed's individual flowers are inconspicuous, they are borne on small, attractive spikes that add interest to the water garden.

Curled pondweed produces both submerged and floating leaves. The submerged leaves are translucent while the floating leaves are more leathery.

Recommended

P. crispus is a trailing, branching plant. The narrow, green or reddish leaves have undulating margins. Spikes of inconspicuous white flowers are borne just above the water's surface in summer.

Daylily
Hemerocallis

Habit: marginal or pondside perennial **Height:** 30 cm–1.2 m (1–4')
Spread: 30 cm–1.2 m (1–4') **Hardiness:** zones 2–8

THERE SEEMS TO be no end to the uses we can find for daylilies.
With their ability to adapt to a wide range of conditions, they give us
ample opportunity to enjoy their beautiful flowers.

Growing

Daylilies grow in any light from **full sun to full shade**, but they produce fewer
flowers in full shade. The soil should be **fertile**, **moist** and **fairly well drained**.
Once established, these plants thrive in almost any conditions.

Division is not required but can be done every three or four years to keep the
plants vigorous and to control their spread.

*More than 12,000 daylily varieties
have been developed, and
hundreds more are added yearly.*

'Stella d'Oro (above); 'Dewey Roquemore' (below)

Tips

Although daylilies are quite drought resistant, wild and naturalized plants are often found growing in drainage ditches. Their high moisture tolerance makes them useful where water overflows after a heavy rain, and they look very much at home next to a water feature, where the arching foliage softens and hides edges well. A long blooming period adds to their popularity.

Recommended

H. Species and **Hybrids** provide a mind-boggling number of hybrids and cultivars that have been developed from a few species of daylilies. The plants form clumps of long, strap-like foliage, with a spread that sometimes exceeds their height. The flowers, held on long stems just above the foliage, range from white and off-white to shades of yellow, orange, pink, red and purple. Each stem has several flowers on it, and each flower opens for just a single day. Some flowers are fragrant and have more than one colour.

Problems & Pests

These generally pest- and problem-free plants are occasionally troubled by rust, *Hemerocallis* gall midges, aphids, spider mites, thrips or slugs.

Dogwood
Cornus

Habit: deciduous pondside tree or shrub **Height:** 1.5–7.5 m (5–25')
Spread: 1.5–7.5 m (5–25') **Hardiness:** zones 2–8

DOGWOODS CAN ADD interest to your water feature and garden all year. Attractive growth habits, colourful stems and interesting flowers are just a few of the features they display throughout the year.

Growing

C. alternifolia grows well in **partial to light shade**. The soil should be of **average to high fertility**, **rich in organic matter**, **neutral to slightly acidic**, **moist** and **fairly well drained**. *C. sericea* has similar requirements but also grows well in **full sun** and tolerates wet soil.

Remove dead, damaged or awkward growth from *C. alternifolia* in spring; it requires little other pruning. *C. sericea*'s stems often lose their colour as they mature, but you can regularly remove up to about one-third of this shrub's stems in spring to make way for colourful new growth. For more drastic rejuvenation, cut the shrub back to within two buds of the ground in spring.

Other species of flowering dogwoods also look attractive near a water feature, but they are not hardy in many Canadian gardens and are more susceptible to problems.

Tips

Dogwoods are often found growing alongside water in the wild. Suitable for a small garden, *C. alternifolia* provides light shade for pondside plants and fish, and is often grown as an attractive tree. *C. sericea* can be included in your bog garden or any area near your pond that tends to remain wet. The bright red stems maintain interest through winter.

Recommended

C. alternifolia (pagoda dogwood) grows 4.5–7.5 m (15–25') tall and spreads 3–7.5 m (10–25'). This native dogwood can be grown as a large, multi-stemmed shrub or as a small, single-stemmed tree. The branches have an attractive layered habit. Early summer brings clusters of small, white flowers. A cultivar with variegated leaves is available. (Zones 3–8)

C. sericea (C. *stolonifera*, red-osier dogwood, red-twig dogwood) grows about 1.5–2 m (5–6¹/₂') tall, spreads up to 3.6 m (12') and bears clusters of

C. *sericea* 'Istanti' (above), C. *alternifolia* (below)

small, white flowers in early summer. A vigorous native shrub with bright red stems, it has foliage that turns red or orange in fall. Cultivars with yellow, orange, red or pink stems are also available.

Problems & Pests

Blight, canker, leaf spot, powdery mildew, root rot, borers, aphids, leafhoppers, scale insects, weevils, nematodes and thrips can trouble many dogwoods, but the species recommended above are less susceptible.

Duckweed

Lemna

Habit: floating perennial **Height:** not applicable **Spread:** indefinite
Hardiness: zones 4–8

DUCKWEED IS A tiny, floating plant that is much enjoyed by fish. It often arrives in your pond with other plants and can be introduced by visiting water birds.

Growing

Duckweeds grow well in **full sun to partial shade**. They simply float at or just below the water's surface, so soil is not required, although *L. trisulca* may sink to the pond bottom in fall and root there until spring, when it floats back up.

If your duckweed is not hardy in your pond, overwinter it indoors in an aquarium.

L. minor (above & below)

Tips

These plants will likely turn up in your pond whether you introduce them or not. You may have to net some out regularly if you don't have fish to keep your duckweed population under control. Duckweed multiplies more rapidly in groups or mats owing to a 'colony' effect. Individual plants multiply more slowly when scattered throughout the pond.

Duckweeds reproduce quickly and rarely suffer from any problems, so you shouldn't have trouble finding another pond owner willing to give you some.

Recommended

L. minor (duckweed) is a tiny, floating plant that usually consists of 2–4 paired leaves. It spreads rapidly and can quickly cover the water's surface unless you have fish that eat it fast enough to limit its spread. Fish can devour duckweed rapidly; some fishkeepers feed it to the fish as a treat.

L. trisulca (ivy-leaved duckweed) is similar to *L. minor*, but it doesn't spread as rapidly. Usually it floats just below the water's surface and has thin, translucent leaves. It sometimes roots at the edge or bottom of the pond, usually in fall but occasionally at other times.

Elephant Ears
Taro
Colocasia

Habit: marginal aquatic or pondside perennial **Height:** 50 cm–2 m (20"–6½')
Spread: 50 cm–2 m (20"–6½') **Hardiness:** tender perennial often grown as
an annual

IF YOUR POND is too small to accommodate a mature elephant ears
plant, it can be grown on dry land in a large container of consistently
moist soil. It will make a striking addition to pondside patios and sitting areas.

C. esculenta 'Black Magic' (above & below)

Growing

Elephant ears grows best in **light to full shade**. The soil should be **fertile, humus rich, slightly acidic** and **moist to wet,** in water up to 20 cm (8") deep.

These plants can easily be brought indoors for winter. Simply place your potted elephant ears in a dish of water in front of a bright window with plenty of space to keep it growing. If you don't have enough space, you can allow the plant to die back in fall and store its tuberous roots in a cool, dry place until spring. In warm places on the West Coast, it may even survive winter outside. Elephant ears can be divided in early spring.

Tips

Plant elephant ears in your pond or in a moist or boggy area next to the water feature, where its large leaves, which can grow to 90 cm (36"), create a tropical appearance. If you plan to lift this plant in fall to be brought indoors, plant it in containers.

Recommended

C. esculenta is a tuberous, warm-climate plant that produces large, heart-shaped leaves. It reaches its maximum size over several seasons. Cultivars with dark purple or red-veined leaves are available.

Problems & Pests

Occasional problems with aphids, bacterial blight, rot, spider mites and whiteflies can occur. However, this plant can withstand heavy insect infestations before showing any symptoms that require treatment.

Eupatorium
Boneset, Joe-Pye Weed
Eupatorium

Habit: pondside perennial **Height:** 1.5–2.1 m (5–7')
Spread: 90 cm–1.5 m (3–5') **Hardiness:** zones 3–8

THESE VIGOROUS, MOUND-FORMING plants attract butterflies and other pollinators to the water garden and are large enough to provide some additional screening and privacy around your pond.

Growing

Eupatoriums prefer **full sun** but tolerate partial shade. The soil should be **fertile** and **moist**. Wet soil is tolerated.

When the plants become overgrown, divide them in spring. Don't put off dividing because the clumps become harder and harder to divide.

Tips

A vigorous root system makes eupatoriums most appropriate for the outside of your pond liner, but they can also be planted in the marginal area or bog area of your water feature.

Recommended

E. cannabinum (hemp agrimony) forms a clump about 1.5 m (5') tall and 1.2–1.5 m (4–5') across with reddish stems. Clusters of white, purple or pink flowers are produced in summer and early fall.

E. maculatum (above & below)

E. maculatum (*E. purpureum*, Joe-Pye weed) forms a large clump 3–4' (90 cm–1.2 m) across with purple-tinged stems and leaves. Clusters of purple flowers are produced in late summer.

Problems & Pests

Rare problems with powdery mildew, fungal leaf spot, rust, aphids, whiteflies and leaf miners can occur.

Eupatoriums need lots of space to grow, so even if the plants are small when you plant them, be sure to leave lots of room for expansion.

Fairy Moss
Mosquito Fern
Azolla

Habit: floating perennial **Height:** not applicable **Spread:** indefinite
Hardiness: zones 7–8

THESE FLOATING PLANTS spread and grow in colonies, forming
lacy patterns of green and red on the surface of your pond.

A. caroliniana (above & below); with *Salvinia* (opposite page)

Growing

Fairy mosses grow well in **full sun to partial shade**. Requiring no soil, they float on the water's surface.

Sometimes they sink to the bottom of the pond in fall to overwinter there, but it's best to scoop a few plants out to overwinter them indoors in an aquarium or even a dish of water.

Tips

Add a small number of plants in late spring to form an attractive shading layer on the surface of the pond. Because these plants are not eaten by fish, you can control their spread by scooping the extra ones out of the pond and putting them in your compost bin. These nitrogen-fixing plants make excellent compost additions.

Recommended

A. caroliniana (*A. filiculoides*) forms a quick-growing, lacy mat of scaly green or reddish foliage on the water's surface.

Problems & Pests

Fairy mosses rarely suffer from any problems, but ducks and other waterfowl may nibble on them from time to time.

Fairy mosses are sometimes called 'mosquito ferns,' but not because they attract mosquitoes. On the contrary, they deter them with their dense growth, which stifles developing larvae.

Floating Heart
Water Snowflake
Nymphoides

Habit: submerged perennial with floating leaves **Height:** not applicable
Spread: indefinite **Hardiness:** zones 5–8

THESE PLANTS ARE admired as much for their attractive floating leaves as for the plentiful small flowers they produce for most of the summer.

Growing

Floating heart grows best in **full sun**. The soil should be a **wet, loamy** pond mix, in water 30–60 cm (12–24") deep. These plants are quite vigorous, and it is often best to plant them in containers to restrict their growth. In a natural or mud-bottomed pond, floating heart can take over as the dominant plant and can be difficult to control.

New plants form at the ends of the long shoots that grow from the base of these plants. Remove these plantlets to prevent excessive spreading, to propagate new plants or to overwinter them indoors in an aquarium in areas where they aren't hardy. Divide your plants as needed in spring or early summer when they have outgrown their containers or growing spaces.

Tips

These plants are appreciated for their long and often prolific blooming period. In a deep part of your home pond, they will provide shade and shelter for your fish and shade out algae at the same time.

N. cristata (above), N. peltata (below)

Recommended

N. cristata (water snowflake) forms a dense, floating mat of small, round leaves that may have red edges or markings. It bears fragrant, white flowers from spring to fall. (Zones 7–8)

N. peltata (floating heart) forms a dense, floating mat of small, round leaves. It produces bright yellow flowers with crinkled edges.

The above recommended species rarely suffer any problems, but as the leaves stack up, the lower ones may turn brown and die. Remove them regularly so they don't rot in your pond.

Flowering Fern

Osmunda

Habit: pondside or bog garden perennial fern **Height:** 75 cm–2 m (30"–6½')
Spread: 60 cm–4 m (2–13') **Hardiness:** zones 2–8

THESE MAGNIFICENT FERNS are welcome additions to any lightly
shaded garden and they lend an air of mystique to a water feature.

*The 'flowers' of flowering ferns
are not actually flowers but
spore-producing sporangia.*

Growing

Flowering ferns prefer **light shade** but tolerate full sun if the soil is consistently wet. The soil should be **fertile, humus rich, acidic** and **moist to wet**.

Divide these plants as needed in fall or early spring to control their spread or to propagate more plants.

Tips

Because these large ferns might overwhelm a small water feature, they are best suited to relatively large ponds and bog gardens, where they can be left to form a large, attractive mass.

Recommended

O. cinnamomea (cinnamon fern) grows 75 cm–1.5 m (30"–5') tall and spreads 60–90 cm (24–36"). Its light green fronds fan out in a circular fashion from a central point. In spring, leafless, cinnamon brown fertile fronds grow straight up from the centre of the plant.

O. regalis (above & below)

O. regalis (royal fern) forms a dense clump of foliage 90 m–2 m (3–6½') tall that spreads 90 cm–4 m (3–13'). The feathery, flower-like fertile fronds that stand out among the light green sterile fronds mature to a rusty brown. (Zones 3–8)

Problems & Pests

Flowering ferns rarely suffer from problems with rust.

Flowering Rush
Swanflower
Butomus

Habit: marginal or bog garden perennial **Height:** 90 cm–1.5 m (3–5')
Spread: 45–60 cm (18–24") **Hardiness:** zones 5–8

THIS CLUMP-FORMING PLANT, with its clusters of attractive summer flowers, grows well in Canadian ponds and enjoys our mild summer weather.

Growing

Flowering rushes grow best in **full sun**. The soil should be **fertile, humus rich** and **muddy**. These plants grow in water up to 20 cm (8") deep.

To keep your plants vigorous and to encourage good flowering, divide them every few years in early spring.

Tips

Flowering rushes are wonderful additions to the edges of your pond, in muddy pockets between the rocks or in containers. They can also be grown in a bog or wet area next to the pond, as long as the soil stays wet.

Flowering rush is a good plant to use when practising your water plant-seeding techniques. Collect seed from the plants in your garden and start them in trays with slightly submerged soil. Once you build your confidence with seeds from your own garden, you will be ready to start the seeds of more difficult plants.

Recommended

B. umbellatus forms a clump of long, narrow, grass-like foliage. In late summer, clusters of fragrant, pink flowers stand out atop long stems.

Problems & Pests

Water lily aphids can occasionally cause trouble.

Flowering rushes make good companions for cattails, and they are often found growing together in the wild.

Frogbit

Hydrocharis • Limnobium

Habit: floating, shallow-water or marginal perennial
Height: not applicable **Spread:** indefinite **Hardiness:** zones 5–8

IF YOU'RE LOOKING for a well-behaved floating plant, you might want to try one of the two frogbits recommended below; they don't spread as quickly as many other available floating plants.

H. morsus-ranae

Growing

Frogbits grow best in **full sun**, in **still, slightly alkaline water**. Although they will grow floating freely, they are more vigorous in shallow water, where the long, trailing roots can reach a muddy pond bottom.

If frogbits are hardy in your area, allow the fall buds to sink to the bottom of the pond and root there in the mud until spring. If they are not hardy, overwinter them indoors in a dish of mud and water in a cool location.

Tips

Introduce these plants to the edge of your pond as free floaters in spring, and they will root themselves in shallow pots with other plants or at the margins of the pond.

Recommended

Hydrocharis morsus-ranae (frogbit) forms a spreading mat of tiny, round leaves up to 5 cm (2") across. This introduction from Europe and northern Africa spreads indefinitely by sending out shoots; new plants form on thier tips. Small, white flowers with yellow centres are produced in summer. (Zones 6–8)

Limnobium spongia (American frogbit) is a completely different species native to North America. It looks and behaves like frogbit but has purple-tinged leaf bottoms and bears insignificant white flowers.

Problems & Pests

Occasional problems with water snails eating the foliage can occur.

With their rounded leaves, these plants are sometimes mistaken for tiny water lilies.

Giant Arum
Skunk Cabbage
Lysichiton

Habit: marginal or pondside perennial **Height:** 60–90 cm (24–36")
Spread: 60 cm–1.2 m (2–4') **Hardiness:** zones 7–8

THESE EARLY-SPRING BLOOMERS will remind you to prepare your pond for another enjoyable summer.

Growing

Giant arums grow well in **full sun to partial shade**. The soil should be **fertile, humus rich** and **wet,** with overlying water up to 10 cm (4") deep.

Giant arums rarely need dividing, but offsets can be removed to propagate new plants.

Tips

Because they are among the first plants to flower in spring, giant arums make nice additions to pond margins. Some people find the flowers' musky odour offensive, so consider planting giant arums on the far side of the pond, and enjoy the sight without the smell.

Recommended

L. americanus (giant yellow arum) grows about 90 cm (36") tall and spreads up to 1.2 m (4'), forming a rosette of glossy green leaves. The yellow-green flower spike, which appears in early spring before the leaves emerge, is sheathed in a bright yellow spathe about 30 cm (12") long.

L. camtschatcensis (giant white arum, white skunk cabbage) has a spread of 60–90 cm (24–36"). It also forms a rosette of glossy green leaves and produces a yellow-green flower spike in early spring before the leaves emerge. The white spathe is about 40 cm (16") long.

Giant arums rarely suffer from problems. In areas where they aren't hardy, plant them in containers and move them to an unheated shed or garage for winter protection. Keep them moist when their pots aren't frozen.

L. americanus (above & below)

Goat's Beard

Aruncus

Habit: pondside or bog garden perennial **Height:** 15 cm–1.8 m (6"–6')
Spread: 30 cm–1.8 m (2–6') **Hardiness:** zones 2–8

GOAT'S BEARD IS a favourite in the perennial garden. Its love of moist soil and its attractive, arching habit make it a favourite of water gardeners too.

Though it can be difficult to tell the two apart, male goat's beard plants have fuzzy flowers, and those on female plants are more pendulous.

Growing

Goat's beard prefers **partial to full shade** but tolerates full sun if the soil stays evenly moist. The soil should be **fertile, humus rich** and **moist**.

Division can be done in spring or fall, but the typical thick root mass can make it difficult.

If you like the appearance of the seedheads, leave them in place; otherwise you can remove them.

Tips

These plants will thrive in the moist soil of a bog garden or in the overflow area of your water feature. A full-sized goat's beard can help blend a small waterfall into the landscape.

A. dioicus (above & below)

Recommended

A. aethusifolius (dwarf Korean goat's beard) forms a low-growing, compact mound 15–40 cm (6–16") tall with a 30 cm (12") spread. Branched spikes of loosely held, creamy white flowers appear in early summer. This plant resembles astilbe and is sometimes sold under that name.

A. dioicus (goat's beard, giant goat's beard) forms a large, bushy, shrublike perennial 90 cm–1.8 m (3–6') tall, with an equal spread. Large plumes of creamy white flowers appear from early through mid-summer, with male and female flowers on separate plants.

Problems & Pests

Occasional problems with tarnished plant bugs are possible.

Golden Club

Orontium

Habit: marginal aquatic perennial **Height:** 30–45 cm (12–18")
Spread: 60–90 cm (24–36") **Hardiness:** zones 5–8

GOLDEN CLUB'S UNUSUAL, EYE-CATCHING flowers and blue-green leaves reach up out of shallow water and are sure to create a conversation piece in your pond.

Golden club to left of elephant ears (*Colocasia*) leaf (above)

Growing

Golden clubs grow best in **full sun** but tolerate even full shade. The soil should be a **wet, loamy** pond mix, in water up to 40 cm (16") deep. These plants, which can be grown in containers or directly in the pond margins, like lots of room so their roots can spread.

Where these plants are not hardy, move them to a deeper part of the pond in fall. They can survive as long as the pond doesn't completely freeze.

Divide the plants as needed in spring when they have outgrown their containers or to control their spread.

Tips

Golden clubs make attractive and unique additions to pond margins. They can also be grown in a bog garden if it is wet enough.

Recommended

O. aquaticum forms a clump of floating or narrow, blue-green aerial leaves. White spikes of tiny, yellow flowers poke up from among the leaves from late spring to mid-summer.

Native to eastern North America, golden clubs rarely suffer from any problems.

Gunnera
Gunnera

Habit: pondside or bog garden perennial **Height:** 1.8–3 m (6–10')
Spread: 1.8–3 m (6–10') **Hardiness:** zones 7–8

IT'S PROBABLY A GOOD thing that these plants are only marginally
hardy in most of Canada. Very few of us have gardens or water features
large enough to accommodate these magnificent beauties.

Growing

Gunneras grow well in **full sun to partial shade**. The soil should be **fertile, humus rich** and **permanently moist**. A **sheltered** location is best, and a winter mulch is recommended.

Although they usually prove too big to divide, gunneras can be propagated by basal cuttings in spring.

Tips

Gunneras enjoy a sheltered bog garden and can be planted at the margin of a pond or near a waterfall, where the giant leaves will hide the water source, giving your pond a mysterious and natural appearance.

Recommended

G. manicata (giant gunnera) forms a huge clump of mammoth-sized leaves up to 2 m (6½') across. The early- or mid-summer clusters of greenish red flowers are often hidden by the foliage.

Problems & Pests

Slugs and snails can be a problem.

This plant is hardy on the West Coast, and gardeners in other warm parts of Canada, such as the East Coast and southern Ontario, sometimes successfully grow gunnera in a sheltered location with a good winter mulch.

Hardy Calla
Water Arum, Bog Arum
Calla

Habit: marginal aquatic, bog garden or pondside perennial
Height: 15–25 cm (6–10") **Spread:** 30–60 cm (12–24")
Hardiness: zones 3–8

THOUGH NOT IMMENSELY showy, hardy callas fill spaces around taller plants and soften the edges of the pond.

Native to much of northern North America, hardy callas prefer cool summer temperatures and rarely experience problems.

Growing

Hardy callas produce the most flowers when grown in **full sun**, but they will tolerate partial shade. The soil should be **humus rich, acidic** and **wet**, in water up to 20 cm (8") deep. They can be grown in containers or planted directly in soil.

Divide hardy callas in spring when they outgrow their containers, or to rejuvenate free-standing clumps.

Tips

Hardy callas make a nice addition to the margins of your pond and can be planted in a very wet part of a bog garden. If grown in containers, they should be kept on the shallowest shelf of the pond.

The fruit is poisonous; take care when children are present so that they don't eat it.

C. palustris (above & below)

Recommended

C. palustris is a low, spreading plant with heart-shaped, glossy leaves and short spikes of green-and-white summer flowers, each surrounded by a white spathe. The fruit ripens to red in fall.

Horsetail

Equisetum

Habit: emergent marginal bog- or pondside perennial **Height:** 15 cm–1.2 m (6"–4')
Spread: indefinite **Hardiness:** zones 3–8

HORSETAIL'S JOINTED STEMS are much appreciated by children who ejnoy breaking the segments apart and rejoining them to form extra-long stems.

Because horsetails can be invasive, grow them in sunken containers, even out of the pond, to restrict their spread. The related E. arvense, *often known as common horsetail, is an invasive weed in much of Canada.*

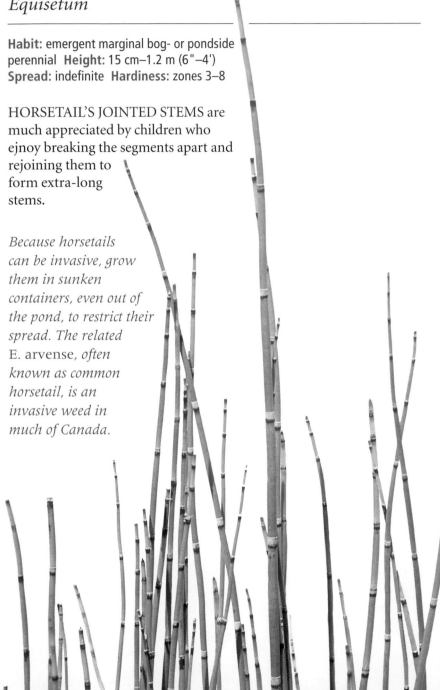

E. hyemale (above), *E. scirpoides* (below)

Growing

Horsetails prefer **full sun.** Grow them in containers of **loamy** pond mix that is **moist to wet,** in water up to 15 cm (6") deep for *E. hyemale* and up to 5 cm (2") deep for *E. scirpoides.*

Divide horsetails as needed in spring or fall when they have outgrown their containers.

Tips

Horsetails can be put in containers and immersed on the shallowest shelf of the pond or buried at the margins or in nearby moist areas. They can also be grown in sunken containers in bog gardens.

Recommended

E. hyemale (common horsetail, scouring-rush) grows up to 1.2 m (4') tall and forms a clump of slender, jointed, reed-like, green stems.

E. scirpoides (dwarf horsetail) grows just 15–20 cm (6–8") tall and forms a clump of very narrow green stems with distinctive brown joints or nodes. (Zones 5–8)

Problems & Pests

Rare problems with rot or blight can occur.

Hosta

Hosta

Habit: pondside perennial **Height:** 20 cm–1.2 m (8"–4')
Spread: 15 cm–1.2 m (6"–4') **Hardiness:** zones 2–8

HOSTAS ARE CONSIDERED by some gardeners to be the ultimate shade plants. Available in a wide variety of leaf shapes, colours and textures, they are a welcome addition to the pondside garden.

Once established, hostas need little attention. Water these hardy plants occasionally and keep them mulched with a rich organic layer.

Growing

Hostas prefer **light to partial shade** but will grow in full shade. Morning sun is preferable to afternoon sun in partial shade situations. The soil should be **fertile, moist** and **fairly well drained,** but these plants adapt to most soil conditions.

Although division is not required, it can be done every few years in early spring or late summer if you want to propagate more plants.

Tips

Hostas are quite drought resistant, but they look so attractive near a water feature that it seems a shame to omit them, especially in shady places. The variation in leaf shapes, sizes and colours adds a lot of interest, and they fit well with ferns and other plants frequently grown in these situations.

Recommended

H. **Species** and **Hybrids** make up a large group of plants grown for their foliage and flowers. In general, they form a dense clump of leaves with rounded bases and pointed tips that can be narrow or broad, with colour ranging from cream through yellow and green to blue, and sometimes variegated. The flower spikes, in white or shades of purple, appear in early, mid- or late summer. Consult your local garden centre to see what is available.

Problems & Pests

Slugs, snails, leaf spot, crown rot and chewing insects such as black vine weevils are all possible problems for hostas. Thick-leaved varieties tend to be more slug resistant.

H. 'Francee' (above & below)

Iris

Iris

Habit: marginal aquatic perennial **Height:** 20 cm–1.5 m (8"–5')
Spread: 60 cm (2') or more **Hardiness:** zones 2–8

FEW GARDENS ARE without at least one iris, but regular gardens often miss out on the iris selections that prefer to grow in water. These classic plants will add a new dimension to your water feature.

A wide variety of plant sizes and flower colours make irises some of the most popular water garden plants. Choose plants with staggered blooming times to enjoy iris flowers all summer.

Growing

Irises grow best in **full sun** but tolerate partial shade. The soil should be **average to fertile, humus rich** and **moist to wet**, in water up to 10 cm (4") deep.

Division is rarely required but can be done between mid-summer and fall when the plants begin to produce fewer flowers or to propagate new plants.

Tips

Popular plants for the margins of a water feature, irises can also be grown in bog gardens and in moist areas around the pond.

I. siberica (above); *I. pseudoacorus* (below)

Recommended

I. pseudoacorus (yellow flag iris) grows 90 cm–1.5 m (3–5') tall and forms clumps of narrow, upright foliage. It bears bright yellow flowers with brown or purple markings in mid- and late summer. Cultivars with variegated leaves or double flowers are available.

I. siberica (Siberian iris) forms clumps of grassy leaves and grows 60 cm–1.2 m (2–4') tall. It normally bears purple flowers in early summer, but cultivars may have pink, blue, white, yellow or red flowers instead.

I. versicolor (blue flag iris) grows 20–80 cm (8–32") tall and spreads 60 cm (2'), forming clumps of upright foliage. This native of eastern North America bears flowers in varied shades of purple in early and mid-summer.

Problems & Pests

Usually problem free, irises have rare problems with iris borers, whiteflies, weevils, thrips, slugs, snails, rot, leaf spot and rust.

Jacob's Ladder
Polemonium

Habit: pondside perennial **Height:** 45–90 cm (18–36")
Spread: 30 cm (12") **Hardiness:** zones 3–8

A PONDSIDE GARDEN makes growing moisture-loving Jacob's
ladder a breeze.

Growing

Jacob's ladders grow well in **partial to very light shade**. The soil should be **fertile, humus rich, moist** and **fairly well drained**. Mulch them in winter if snow cover is undependable in your garden and if your temperatures regularly drop below −18° C (0° F).

Deadhead your plants to prolong blooming and to reduce self-seeding. Division is not required but can be done in fall if more plants are desired.

Tips

Include these striking plants in your pondside garden or at the edges of a bog garden, but avoid planting them in standing water.

Recommended

P. caeruleum forms a dense clump of basal foliage. Upright, leafy stems hold clusters of purple flowers in late spring and summer. Cultivars with white flowers or foliage with off-white margins are also available.

Problems & Pests

Powdery mildew, leaf spot and rust cause occasional problems.

Jacob's ladder gets its name from the neat, dense, ladder-like formation of its leaflets.

P. caeruleum 'Alba' (above)

'Bressingham Purple' (below)

Kaffir Lily

Schizostylis

Habit: pondside perennial **Height:** 30–60 cm (12–24")
Spread: 30 cm (12") **Hardiness:** zones 7–8

THESE EXOTIC PLANTS are admired for their gladiolus-like flower spikes, which make a welcome appearance in late summer or fall.

Kaffir lilies are generally problem free. It is a good idea to mulch them in winter, however, even on the West Coast, where they are hardy.

Growing

Kaffir lilies grow best in **full sun**. The soil should be of **average fertility, moist** and **well drained**.

Where these plants are not hardy, grow them in sunken containers and bring them indoors for winter. Zone 6 gardeners may successfully over-winter them with a thick layer of mulch.

Divide your plants in spring if you want to propagate them.

Tips

Kaffir lilies bring a welcome burst of colour to the pondside in fall, when red and pink flowers are less common. Use them in moist (but not soggy) areas near your water feature, perhaps near a sitting area where you can enjoy the flowers on a warm day.

S. coccinea (all photos)

Recommended

S. coccinea forms a clump of grassy foliage and bears spikes or clusters of red flowers in fall. Some cultivars have pink or white flowers.

Katsura-Tree

Cercidiphyllum

Habit: deciduous pondside tree **Height:** 3–21 m (10–70') **Spread:** 12–21 m (40–70') **Hardiness:** zones 4–8

KATSURA-TREE IS A BEAUTIFUL addition to any garden. It looks great near a water feature where it can provide some shade for pondside plantings.

C. japonicum *is the largest native deciduous tree in Japan and China, where it reaches heights of 40 m (130') in the wild.*

Growing

Katsura-trees grow well in **full sun to partial shade**. The soil should be **fertile, humus rich, neutral to acidic, moist** and **well drained**. Water regularly during dry spells for the first few years after planting; this will help the tree establish quickly.

Pruning is not required. Damaged branches can be removed at any time, and awkward branches can be removed in spring.

Tips

Katsura-trees make beautiful, trouble-free additions to your pondside plantings. Their slow growth makes them suitable for small gardens, but keep in mind their size at maturity. A weeping specimen is an ideal complement to any water feature.

Recommended

C. japonicum is a slow-growing, pyramidal tree that grows 12–21 m (40–70') tall, with an equal or greater, rounded to spreading habit that develops as it matures. In fall, the heart-shaped, blue-green leaves turn shades of yellow, orange and red and develop a spicy scent. Grafted specimens can be hard to find, but **'Pendulum'** is often available. It has a drooping habit and is often used to create a weeping standard. Its pendulous branches are usually grafted to a 3–4.5 m (10–15') trunk. When mature, it resembles a waterfall tumbling down a rocky slope and makes a stunning specimen.

Katsura-trees are usually free of problems.

When changing into their fall colours, Kastsura-tree leaves emit a spicy aroma

Lady Fern
Japanese Painted Fern
Athyrium

Habit: perennial pondside fern **Height:** 30–60 cm (12–24")
Spread: 30–60 cm (12–24") **Hardiness:** zones 3–8

THOUGH ALL FERNS are considered decorative, lady fern fronds
have beautiful colours that stand out in a crowd.

*With its colourful foliage, lady
fern will brighten shaded areas
near your pond.*

Growing

Lady ferns and painted ferns grow well in **full shade, partial shade** or **light shade**. The soil should be of **average fertility, humus rich, acidic** and **moist** (but not soggy).

Although it is rarely required, division can be done in spring if you want to propagate more plants.

Tips

Unlike some ferns, the recommended species below are relatively well behaved, forming attractive masses of foliage without growing out of control. Plant them on a moist, shady bank or in a hollow next to your water feature. They can also be included at the edges of a bog garden in moist but not soggy soil.

Recommended

A. filix-femina (lady fern) forms a dense clump of lacy fronds that can spread 60 cm (2'). Cultivars can feature variable foliage or dwarf characteristics.

A. niponicum cultivar (above),
A. niponicum var. *pictum* (below)

A. niponicum var. *pictum* 'Metallicum' (Japanese painted fern) forms a clump of dark green fronds with a silvery or reddish metallic sheen. It can spread 30 cm (12"). Other cultivars of var. *pictum* offer different foliage colours. (Zones 4–8)

The species recommended above rarely suffer from any problems.

Ligularia
Giant Groundsel
Ligularia

Habit: pondside or bog garden perennial **Height:** 90 cm–1.8 m (3–6')
Spread: 90 cm–1.2 m (3–4') **Hardiness:** zones 2–8

THESE BOLD PLANTS are well suited to a pondside garden where they can be used to shade the margins and soften the edges of the water feature.

Ligularias are long-lived perennials. Their flowers make interesting additions to a cut-flower arrangement.

Growing

Ligularias grow best in **light to partial shade** with **protection** from the afternoon sun. The soil should be of **average to high fertility, humus rich** and **consistently moist**.

Division is rarely, if ever, required, but it can be done in spring or fall to propagate a desirable cultivar.

Tips

These bold plants are excellent additions to your pondside or bog garden.

Ligularias that wilt during the day and perk up again at night are getting too much sun. Move them to a cooler, shadier location, even if their soil is moist.

Recommended

L. dentata (bigleaf ligularia, golden groundsel) forms a clump of rounded, heart-shaped leaves 90 cm– 1.5 m (3–5') tall. It bears clusters of orange-yellow flowers above the foliage in summer and early fall. Cultivars with purple-tinged leaves are available. (Zones 3–8)

L. wilsoniana (giant groundsel) forms a spreading clump of large, rounded or heart-shaped leaves 1.5–1.8 m (5–6') tall. Large spikes bearing yellow flowers are produced in mid-summer.

Problems & Pests

These plants have no serious problems, but slugs can damage young foliage.

L. wilsoniana (above), *L. dentata* (below)

Lizard's Tail

Saururus

Habit: marginal aquatic perennial **Height:** 20–60 cm (8–24") **Spread:** 60 cm (up to 24") **Hardiness:** zones 4–8

LIZARD'S TAIL IS ONE of the few water feature plants that thrive in a shaded pond.

Lizard's tails rarely have any problems; even when they are grown in full shade, flowering is only slightly reduced.

S. cernuus (above & below)

Growing

Lizard's tails grow well in all light conditions, from **full sun to full shade**. The soil should be a **wet, loamy** pond mix, in water 5–20 cm (2–8") deep. They can be grown in containers or directly in the pond. Divide the clumps in spring when they have outgrown their containers or to propagate more plants.

Tips

Lizard's tails are attractive and well-behaved plants that grow happily in the margins of your pond or in a very soggy bog garden.

Recommended

S. **cernuus** forms a clump of heart-shaped leaves and bears curving spikes of fragrant, white flowers in mid-summer.

Lobelia
Cardinal Flower
Lobelia

Habit: emergent, marginal aquatic or pondside perennial
Height: 20 cm–1.2 m (8"–4') **Spread:** 30–60 cm (12–24")
Hardiness: zones 4–8; cultivars may be less or more hardy

LOBELIA ADDS A bright splash of colour and attracts hummingbirds, butterflies and other pollinators to your water feature.

Growing

Lobelias grow best in **full sun to light shade.** For *L. cardinalis*, the soil should be **fertile, slightly acidic** and **moist,** and it should be mulched in winter. *L. dortmanna* prefers a **wet, loamy** pond mix, in up to 10 cm (4") of water, either in a container or planted directly in the pond.

Vividly coloured lobelia flowers create stunning reflections on the surface of still water.

Deadhead your lobelias to prolong blooming, but leave a few spent flowers in place to go to seed.

Divide the plants every two to three years in fall to keep them growing vigorously. They are often short-lived, but they tend to self-seed and replace themselves with new plants.

Tips

L. cardinalis prefers the moist borders around a pond, stream or waterfall, whereas *L. dortmanna* likes to be grown in the moist margins at the edge of the pond. Both types can be grown in bog gardens.

Recommended

L. cardinalis (cardinal flower) grows 60 cm–1.2 m (2–4') tall, forming an upright clump of bronze-green leaves. It bears spikes of bright red flowers from summer to fall.

L. cardinalis (above & below)

L. dortmanna (water lobelia) is an emergent or marginal aquatic perennial that grows up to 60 cm (2') tall and spreads 30 cm (12"). It forms rosettes of foliage at the water's surface. Drooping clusters of light blue or light purple flowers are held above the water in summer.

L. x *speciosa* (hybrid cardinal flower, hybrid lobelia) grows 20–90 cm (8–36") tall and is the most vigorous of the lobelias, but hardiness can vary from hybrid to hybrid. The flowers, in shades of red, pink, purple and white, appear in mid- to late summer.

Problems & Pests

Rare problems with slugs, snails, rust, smut and leaf spot can occur.

Loosestrife

Lysimachia

Habit: pondside perennial **Height:** 5–90 cm (2–36") **Spread:** 45 cm (18") to indefinite **Hardiness:** zones 2–8

LOOSESTRIFE, WITH ITS varied habits, makes a useful clump-forming plant or a groundcover around the edges of a pond or stream.

*The invasive purple loosestrife (*Lythrum salicaria) *is not related to the* Lysimachias.

Growing

Loosestrife grows well in **full sun to partial shade**. The soil should be of **average fertility, humus rich** and **moist** (but not soggy).

Divide the plants in spring or fall to control their spread. The trailing stems of *L. nummularia* can also be cut back if they begin to spread farther than you would like.

Tips

L. clethroides is an attractive and care-free addition to the moist pondside border, where it self-seeds and pops up here and there. *L. nummularia* is a good plant to include among the rocks around your pond or next to your waterfall, where its trailing stems will spread over the edges and may even stretch out into the water.

L. clethroides (above),
Yellow-flowered *L. nummularia* (below)

Recommended

L. clethroides (gooseneck loosestrife) grows 60–90 cm (24–36") tall, with an equal spread. In mid-summer to early fall, this upright, spreading plant produces flowers on curved, tapered spikes that gradually grow upright as the flowers open.

L. nummularia (creeping Jenny) grows 5–10 cm (2–4") tall. This prostrate, spreading plant with trailing stems bears bright yellow flowers in summer. A popular yellow-leaved cultivar is frequently available.

Problems & Pests

Rare problems with rust and leaf spot can occur.

Lotus

Nelumbo

Habit: emergent aquatic perennial **Height:** 60 cm–2 m (2–6½')
Spread: indefinite **Hardiness:** zones 4–8

GETTING A LOTUS to bloom in most parts of Canada is a bit of a
water gardener's Holy Grail. Very few Canadian ponds or
gardens receive the temperatures these exotic plants
require to flower. This doesn't prevent us from
trying, though.

N. nucifera 'Sacred Pink' (above), *N. nucifera* 'Mrs. Perry Slocum' (below)

Growing

Lotuses prefer **full sun** but tolerate partial shade. The soil should be a **wet, fertile, loamy** pond mix, in 30–60 cm (12–24") of water for full-sized plants or 15–25 cm (6–10") for dwarf plants.

Lotuses can be grown directly in the pond or in containers. Rather than immediately submerging these plants to their maximum depth, raise the water level gradually as the plants fill in over spring and summer. **Sheltered** locations out of the wind are preferable. These heavy feeders may need **fertilizing** twice a month in summer when they are growing vigorously.

When your lotuses outgrow their containers, divide them in spring. Be as gentle as you can because they resent having their delicate roots

The lotus is sacred to both Hindus and Buddhists and a wealth of mythology surrounds this plant and its lovely flowers.

disturbed. Even the slightest crack in the tuber can be fatal to the plant.

Although these plants are quite cold hardy, take extra care if they are in containers. You can gradually reduce water levels in fall and move the plants to a cool, frost-free place indoors for winter. If your pond doesn't freeze solid, lower them to the bottom in fall so they can remain below the winter ice.

Tips

Lotuses are actually quite easy to grow and almost any water gardener can enjoy a lush green plant. Getting a plant to flower is the tricky part. The biggest requirement is heat—water temperatures must stay at about 27° C (80° F) for several weeks to initiate blooming. However, most ponds in Canadian gardens don't get this warm, at least not for several weeks at a time, and for the health of

N. nucifera flower buds (above); 'Sacred Pink' (below)

fish and other plants in your pond, you wouldn't want them to.

The best way to get lotuses to bloom is to grow them in containers on a patio or near a pond. Several dwarf varieties well suited to patio-sized containers are available. Popular containers include lined half-barrels and attractive lined planters. Keep your lotuses in a warm, sunny location and add water as necessary; evaporation and the plant's water needs can cause significant water loss on warm days.

A lotus flower lasts for three days, opening each morning and closing by mid-afternoon. Each day, the flower becomes lighter in colour, changing, for example, from pink to yellow to white.

Recommended

N. lutea (American lotus, water chinquapin) grows up to 2 m (6½') tall and forms a clump of stems topped with large, round leaves that stand above the water and grow to 50 cm (20") across. It is native to North America and produces yellow flowers in summer.

N. nucifera (sacred lotus) grows 90 cm–1.5 m (3–5') tall and forms a clump of stems topped with round, wavy-edged leaves up to 80 cm (32") across. It bears fragrant flowers in shades of pink or white in summer. Many cultivars are available, including several dwarf cultivars that grow about 60 cm (2') tall.

Problems & Pests

Rare problems with spider mites, whiteflies and leaf spot can occur.

'Sacred Pink' (above); 'Mrs. Perry Slocum' (below)

Lotus seedpods are popular for use in flower arrangements.

Lungwort
Pulmonaria

Habit: pondside perennial **Height:** 15–45 cm (6–18")
Spread: 30–45 cm (12–18") **Hardiness:** zones 2–8

THIS MOISTURE-LOVING plant has happily made the crossover
from the perennial garden to the pondside garden. Attractive flowers
and decorative foliage make lungwort a winner.

*Lungworts create an attractive
contrast with hostas, columbines,
ferns and other pondside
favourites.*

Growing

Lungworts prefer **partial to full** shade. The soil should be **fertile, humus rich, moist** and **fairly well drained**. Rot can occur in very wet soil.

Divide your plants in early summer after flowering or in fall. Newly planted divisions should be well watered to help them reestablish.

Deadhead lungworts lightly after flowering to keep them tidy and show off their fabulous foliage.

Tips

Lungworts make attractive and interesting groundcovers next to ponds and streams.

The leaves of this plant are edible. If it's planted close enough to the pond, you may find that your fish like to nibble on the leaves while they rest in the shade of your lungwort.

Recommended

P. **Species** and **Hybrids** produce spring flowers, usually in shades of blue or purple, but white and pink are also available. Once the flowers are finished, the low mounds of foliage create equally interesting displays of spotted, splotched, margined or silvery leaves.

Problems & Pests

These plants are generally problem free but may become susceptible to powdery mildew if the soil dries out for extended periods. Remove and destroy damaged leaves.

P. saccharata (above)

Maidenhair Fern
Northern Maidenhair
Adiantum

Habit: pondside perennial fern **Height:** 30–60 cm (12–24")
Spread: 30–60 cm (12–24") **Hardiness:** zones 2–8

NO WATER FEATURE should be without this delicate and graceful fern. It is well behaved and hardy.

A. pedatum (above & below)

Growing

Maidenhair ferns grow well in **light to partial shade** and tolerate full shade. The soil should be of **average fertility, humus rich** and **moist.**

Although maidenhair ferns rarely need dividing, you can do so in spring to propagate more plants.

Tips

These lovely ferns happily grace the shady edge of any pond and can also be included in a moist, but not water-logged, part of a bog garden.

Recommended

A. pedatum forms a spreading mound of delicate, arching fronds. The light green leaflets stand out against black stems, and the whole plant turns bright yellow in fall.

A. pedatum *rarely suffers from problems. Most of the many other species of maidenhair ferns are not hardy in Canadian gardens and are better suited as houseplants or for greenhouses.*

Manna Grass

Glyceria

Habit: emergent or marginal aquatic perennial grass   **Height:** 30–90 cm (12–36")
Spread: indefinite   **Hardiness:** zones 4–8

WITH THE RECENT increased interest in including grasses in gardens, it seems appropriate that there should be a few reserved for water gardeners. Manna grass needs moist soil and growing conditions that are difficult to replicate without a pond.

Manna grasses thrive in relatively deep water and can be used to shelter and shade fish near the middle of an average-sized pond.

G. maxima 'Variegata' (above), *G. maxima* (below)

Growing

Manna grasses grow best in **full sun**. Use a **moist to wet, loamy** pond mix, in water up to 60 cm (2') deep.

Divide these grasses as needed when they have outgrown their containers or to control their spread if you planted them directly in the pond.

Tips

Manna grasses look attractive when their leaves emerge from the water, but they can also live in moist areas near the pond or in a bog garden.

Recommended

G. maxima (*G. aquatica*) forms a clump of dark green leaves. Newly emerging leaves are tinged with pink.

The cultivar **'Variegata'** (variegated manna grass) is most frequently grown. It has green-, yellow- and white-striped leaves.

Problems & Pests

Typical problems include fungal leaf spot, rust and smut.

Maple

Acer

Habit: deciduous pondside tree **Height:** 1.8–7.5 m (6–25')
Spread: 1.8–7.5 m (6–25') or more **Hardiness:** zones 2–8

MANY CANADIANS FEEL a sentimental attachment to maple trees and are happy to include at least one in their gardens. The smaller species recommended here are suitable for growing next to a pond without creating dense shade or occupying too much space.

Appreciated for its versatility of size, shape and leaf colour, A. palmatum is possibly one of the most popular small trees for waterside gardens.

Growing

Both maple species recommended below grow well in **full sun to partial shade**. The soil should be **fertile, high in organic matter, moist** and **fairly well drained**.

These maples respond well to pruning, but little is required. Remove dead, damaged, and awkward growth as needed.

Tips

These trees are often described as resembling artwork or sculpture. Gardeners often thin out some of the growth so that the attractive bark can be more easily seen. The trees can be pruned to encourage unusual growth patterns and to create a unique focal point for your waterside garden. Both species are also popular for creating bonsai specimens. Even when left to grow naturally, these attractive trees provide interest year-round.

Recommended

A. ginnala (Amur maple) makes an excellent alternative to the less-hardy Japanese maple. It can be grown as a large, multi-stemmed shrub or as a beautiful, small, single-stemmed tree. The samaras (winged seeds) turn red in late summer, creating a striking display against the dark green leaves, which turn bright red in fall.

A. palmatum (Japanese maple) is one of the most popular trees for small gardens. The many available cultivars offer tree, bushy, spreading and weeping forms. Dwarf and slow-growing cultivars grow 1.8–4.5 m (6–15') tall and spread up to 4.5 m (15'). Cultivars may have red, purple,

A. ginnala 'Bailey Compact' (above)

green or yellow foliage, and their leaves may be so deeply lobed and divided that they appear lacy or fern-like. Check with your local garden centre for availability. (Zones 5–8)

Problems & Pests

Aphids, borers, caterpillars, leaf-hoppers, scale insects, anthracnose, canker, leaf spot and *Verticillium* wilt can affect maples. Chlorosis (leaf yellowing) caused by manganese or iron deficiency can occur in alkaline soils. Adequate watering prevents leaf scorch on young trees during hot, dry weather.

A. palmatum var. *dissectum* (below)

Marsh Marigold

Caltha

Habit: marginal or bog perennial **Height:** 20–40 cm (8–16")
Spread: 25–50 cm (10–20") **Hardiness:** zones 2–8

MARSH MARIGOLDS ARE harbingers of spring in the water garden. They offer glossy green leaves and bright yellow flowers when most other plants have barely started to sprout.

Marsh marigolds go dormant in mid-summer and many have been dug up and thrown out by gardeners who assume that they are dead.

Growing

Marsh marigolds grow well in **full sun to partial shade**. The soil should be of **average fertility** and **moist to wet**, with up to 15 cm (6") of water. These plants often die back in summer as the weather heats up. Don't dig them up; they will reappear next spring.

Divide your plants every two or three years, after flowering has finished in spring.

Tips

Best suited to marginal areas, marsh marigolds can also be planted in bog areas or in any wet areas near your pond or stream. Try planting groups of them all around your water feature. As they die back for the season, other summer plants will fill in around them. Native to Canada, they are also a good choice for a naturalized water feature.

C. palustris var. *alba* (above), *C. palustris* (below)

Recommended

C. palustris forms a low mound of heart-shaped leaves. Yellow flowers appear in spring. Cultivars with double flowers or white flowers are also available.

Problems & Pests

Powdery mildew and rust usually only cause trouble in plants that aren't getting enough water.

Masterwort

Astrantia

Habit: pondside perennial **Height:** 30–90 cm (12–36") **Spread:** 45 cm (18")
Hardiness: zones 4–8

MASTERWORT HAS BECOME more common with the increasing
popularity of water gardens; many of us previously had trouble keeping the soil moist enough for this plant to thrive.

*With their stiff, papery bracts,
masterwort
flower clusters
are useful
additions to
fresh or dried flower
arrangements.*

Growing

Masterworts prefer **light to partial shade** but tolerate full sun in moist soil. The soil should be **fertile, humus rich** and **moist**.

Deadhead your masterworts to reduce self-seeding. Divide them in spring or fall to propagate and keep the clumps growing vigorously.

Tips

Their unusual flowers and lobed foliage make masterworts good additions to the waterside garden. Use them at the edge of a bog area or anywhere that stays moist but not soggy.

Recommended

A. major (great masterwort) forms a clump of deeply lobed foliage. All summer long, it bears clusters of pink, green, red or purple flowers surrounded by stiff green, white or pink bracts. Cultivars are available, but only with flowers of particular colours.

A. major (all photos); 'Sunningdale Gold' (left), 'Rubra' (above), 'Hadspen's Blood' (below)

Problems & Pests

Rare problems with mould, mildew, slugs and aphids can occur.

Meadow Rue

Thalictrum

Habit: pondside perennial **Height:** 60 cm –1.5 m (2–5')
Spread: 60 cm–1.5 m (2–5') **Hardiness:** zones 3–8

THE LACY LEAVES and loosely clustered flowers of meadow rue
have an airy, cooling appearance that is always appreciated during
the heat of summer.

T. delavayi 'Hewitt's Double' (opposite page & above), *T. aquilegifolium* (below)

Growing

Meadow rues prefer **light to partial shade** but tolerate full sun in moist soil. The soil should be **humus rich, moist** and **fairly well drained**.

Division is not required for these slow-growing plants. If you want to propagate more plants, divide them in spring as the leaves begin to develop. Keep in mind, though, that they resent having their roots disturbed and will take a long time to recover.

Tips

These plants make elegant additions to the plantings around your water feature. Include them in the bog garden or water overflow area, but don't let them stand in water.

Recommended

T. aquilegifolium (columbine meadow rue) forms an upright mound 60–90 cm (24–36") tall with an equal spread. It is named for its leaves, which resemble those of columbines. Fluffy purple flower clusters are borne in early summer. Cultivars with darker purple or white flowers are available.

T. delavayi **'Hewitt's Double'** forms a clump of narrow stems that spreads about 60 cm (2') and usually needs staking. It bears loose clusters of tiny, purple flowers for most of summer.

Problems & Pests

Rare problems with powdery mildew, rust, smut and leaf spot can occur.

Meadowsweet

Filipendula

Habit: marginal or pondside perennial **Height:** 60 cm–2.4 m (2–8')
Spread: 60 cm–1.2 m (2–4') **Hardiness:** zones 3–8

THE WONDERFULLY FRAGRANT plumes of meadowsweet flowers make this plant worth including at the edge of the water feature.

The flowers of F. ulmaria
*were once used to
flavour meads
and ales.*

Growing

Meadowsweets prefer **partial to light shade** but tolerate full sun in adequately moist soil. The soil should be **fertile, deep, humus rich** and **moist**. They can grow right at the water's edge but prefer not to be submerged.

Deadhead your meadowsweets if you don't like the appearance of the brown seedheads or if you find too many seedlings sprouting. Divide the plants in spring or fall to propagate them and keep them growing vigorously. You may need a sharp knife because they develop thick roots.

Tips

These attractive plants can be mass-planted at the edge of your water feature or used as individual specimens in plant groupings. The plumes of fragrant flowers attract bees, butterflies and other pollinators.

Recommended

F. rubra 'Venusta' forms a large, spreading clump 1.8–2.4 m (6–8') tall, with a spread of 1.2 m (4'). The

F. ulmaria (above & below)

showy, mid-summer clusters of fragrant, bright pink flowers fade to light pink in fall. The naturally occurring species has lighter pink flowers.

F. ulmaria forms a clump of leafy stems, grows 60–90 cm (24–36") tall and spreads 60 cm (2'). It bears large clusters of fragrant, creamy white flowers in summer. Cultivars with double flowers or variegated leaves are also available.

Problems & Pests

Problems with powdery mildew, rust and leaf spot can occur.

Monkey Flower
Mimulus

Habit: marginal or pondside annual **Height:** 15–30 cm (6–12")
Spread: 30 cm (12") **Hardiness:** half-hardy or tender annual

IT IS ALWAYS useful to include annual plants that provide colour and
fill spaces around perennials and shrubs that haven't reached their
mature size. Monkey flower is ideal for this purpose; it loves the moist
conditions of a pond.

Two other species—M. luteus *with
yellow flowers and M.* ringens *with pale
mauve or blue flowers—are hardy
perennials in parts of Canada but
don't flower as prolifically
as the hybrids. They
both grow in
shallow
water.*

Growing

Monkey flowers prefer **light to partial shade,** with **protection** from the afternoon sun. Too much sun can make them straggly and unattractive. The soil should be **fertile, humus rich** and **moist**—don't let it dry out.

Tips

These flowering annuals can be used to add colour around the edges of your water feature or to brighten a bog garden. In ideal conditions, they will bloom for most of summer.

Recommended

M. x *hybridus* (hybrid monkey flower) is a bushy, low, branching plant. The many cultivars offer flowers in bright and pastel shades ranging from orange, yellow and cream to burgundy, pink and red. Bicolours are also available.

M. x *hybridus* 'Mystic Mix' (above)

Problems & Pests

Downy mildew, powdery mildew, grey mould, whiteflies, spider mites and aphids can cause occasional problems.

Monkshood

Aconitum

Habit: pondside perennial **Height:** 90 cm–1.5 m (3–5')
Spread: 30–60 cm (12–24") **Hardiness:** zones 2–8

COPIOUS BRIGHT BLUE
or purple flowers will give a
visual cooling effect enhanced
by the sound of running water as
you enjoy the hot days of mid-
and late summer.

*Wear gloves or wash
your hands
thoroughly after
handling monkshoods
because the sap is
poisonous.*

Growing

Monkshoods grow best in **light to partial shade**. The soil should be **fertile, humus rich** and **moist**. Some tall monkshoods need to be staked. Peony hoops placed around young plants will be hidden as the plants fill in over summer.

Because these plants resent having their roots disturbed, division is not recommended.

Tips

Tall, elegant monkshoods are at home in the moist soil of a bog garden or along the edges of a pond or stream. They perform best in gardens where the weather stays a bit cool in summer.

Recommended

A. x *cammarum* (cammarum hybrids) grow about 90 cm (36") tall and spread about 60 cm (2'). With their strong stems, they often don't need staking. The flowers are borne in mid- and late summer. Two popular cultivars in this group are **'Bicolor,'** with blue-and-white flowers, and **'Bressingham Spire,'** with dark purple-blue flowers.

A. napellus (common monkshood) grows 90 cm–1.5 m (3–5') tall and spreads 30–45 cm (12–18"). This erect plant, which forms a basal mound of finely divided foliage, may flop over unless it is staked. It bears dark purple-blue flowers in mid- and late summer.

Problems & Pests

Problems with aphids, root rot, stem rot, powdery mildew, downy mildew, wilt and rust can occur.

A. napellus (opposite page), 'Bicolor' (above & below)

Mountain Laurel
Kalmia, Calico Bush
Kalmia

Habit: evergreen pondside or bog shrub **Height:** 15 cm–4.5 m (6"–15')
Spread: 15 cm–4.5 m (6"–15') **Hardiness:** zones 2–8

THESE NORTH AMERICAN natives produce clusters of beautiful, cup-shaped flowers in shades of pink, purple, red or white.

Wash your hands after handling K. latifolia; *ingesting any parts, including the sap, can cause stomach upset.*

Growing

These laurels prefer **partial to light shade** but tolerate full sun in consistently moist soil. The soil should be **humus rich, acidic** and **moist** (*K. latifolia*) or wet (*K. microphylla* and *K. polifolia*).

Little pruning is required. Simply remove dead, damaged and awkward growth in spring. To keep your laurels tidy and encourage good flower production the following year, deadhead them once flowering is finished.

Tips

Commonly available in garden centres, *K. latifolia* makes an attractive choice for moist areas surrounding your water feature. *K. microphylla* and *K. polifolia* are better suited to water garden cultivation and can be planted in the moist, marginal area around your pond or in a bog garden, but they are harder to find.

Recommended

K. latifolia (mountain laurel) is a bushy shrub that grows 2.1–4.5 m (7–15') tall with an equal spread, and can be trained to resemble a small tree. It has glossy green leaves and bears clusters of pink or white flowers from late spring to mid-summer. Many cultivars, usually with flowers in specific colours, are available. (Zones 4–8)

K. microphylla (western laurel) and *K. polifolia* (eastern bog laurel) are two similar, low-growing plants that are native to wet sites west and east of the Rocky Mountains respectively. *K. microphylla* grows 15–60 cm (6–24") tall and spreads 15–30 cm

K. latifolia 'Ostbo Red' (above), *K. latifolia* (below)

(6–12"), bearing pink flower in late spring and early summer. *K. polifolia* grows up to 60 cm (2') tall and spreads 90 cm (36"). It bears pink or purple-pink flowers in mid- to late spring.

Problems & Pests

Rare problems with leaf spot, scale insects, powdery mildew, lace bugs and borers can occur.

Obedient Plant

Physostegia

Habit: pondside perennial **Height:** 60 cm–1.2 m (2–4') **Spread:** 60 cm (2') or more **Hardiness:** zones 2–8

ONCE PLANTED NEXT to your pond, obedient plant will proba-bly start to show up in other spots around your pond and elsewhere in your garden.

Obedient plants can become invasive. Planting them in sunken containers will help prevent excessive spreading.

Growing

Obedient plants prefer **full sun** but tolerate partial to light shade. The soil should be of **average fertility** and **moist**.

Divide them in early to mid-spring every few years to control their spread.

Tips

These plants are well suited to the moist borders around your pond and will spread happily in a bog garden. Late-summer flowers are always a welcome sight.

Recommended

P. virginiana has a spreading root system from which upright stems sprout. It bears spikes of purple, pink or white flowers from mid-summer

P. virginiana (all photos)

to fall. The many available cultivars include dwarf plants, less invasive selections and plants with variegated foliage.

Problems & Pests

Rare problems with rust, slugs and snails are possible.

Ornamental Rhubarb

Rheum

Habit: pondside perennial **Height:** 1.8–2.4 m (6–8')
Spread: 90 cm–2 m (3–6½') **Hardiness:** zones 3–8

MOST OF US are familiar with the common edible rhubarb, but there are also many exciting decorative rhubarbs that will add dramatic flair to your pondside plantings with brightly coloured or deeply divided foliage and large clusters of tiny flowers.

Ornamental rhubarbs are good for providing large leaves in gardens where gunneras aren't hardy.

Growing

Ornamental rhubarbs grow well in **full sun to partial shade**. The soil should be **fertile, humus rich** and **moist**. During hot weather, they may go dormant.

When flowering becomes reduced, divide your ornamental rhubarbs in early spring to control plant spread or to propagate more plants. Dead-head the plants to keep them looking tidy and mulch them with compost each fall.

Tips

Planted at the water's edge, ornamental rhubarbs make majestic feature plants. Allow the leaves to stretch out over the pond but don't allow dead leaves to collect and rot in the water in fall. Alternatively, include them at the edges of a bog garden.

Ornamental rhubarbs are not edible. If you would prefer edible stems paired with somewhat ornamental leaves, plant the common rhubarb (*R.* x *hybridum*) beside your pond.

Recommended

R. palmatum forms a clump of broad, toothed leaves on sturdy stems. It bears large, plumy clusters of green or red flowers in early summer. **'Atrosanguineum'** ('Atropur-pureum') has emerging leaves of red or purple that mature to dark green over summer. **Var.** *tanguticum* grows 1.8 m (6') tall with an equal spread. It has jagged-edged, reddish green leaves that turn dark green or tinge purple over summer and large clusters of white, pink or red flowers.

Problems & Pests

Rare problems with rot and rust can occur.

Ostrich Fern

Matteuccia

Habit: pondside perennial fern **Height:** 90 cm–1.5 m (3–5')
Spread: 30–90 cm (12–36") or more **Hardiness:** zones 1–8

THESE POPULAR, CLASSIC ferns are appreciated as much
for their delicious emerging spring fronds as for their
stately, vase-shaped habits.

Growing

Ostrich ferns prefer **partial to light shade** but tolerate full shade. The soil should be **average to fertile, humus rich, neutral to acidic** and **moist**.

If you want to pass plants on to friends and neighbours, established clumps of these hearty spreaders can be divided as needed in spring when growth begins to emerge.

Tips

The edges of many natural streams are graced with these ferns, which will grow just as happily in a moist, shady spot next to your pond. Given time, a clump can spread well beyond any space you may have provided for it.

Recommended

M. struthiopteris (*M. pennsylvanica*) forms a circular cluster of slightly arching, green fronds. Stiff, brown fertile fronds stick up in the centre of the cluster in late summer and persist through winter.

M. struthiopteris (above & below)

Known as fiddleheads and considered a delicacy, the tightly coiled, new spring fronds taste delicious lightly steamed and served with butter. Remove the bitter, reddish brown papery coating before preparing them. Ostrich ferns are generally free of problems.

Papyrus
Paper Reed
Cyperus

Habit: marginal aquatic perennial **Height:** 30 cm–1.5 m (1–5')
Spread: 40–90 cm (16–36") **Hardiness:** zones 6–8

THOUGH THE FLOWERS of papyrus aren't very showy, they are produced in attractive, umbrella-shaped clusters that make them interesting additions to the shallows of your pond.

Papyruses are popular with barrel-pond gardeners who often have to overwinter all their pond plants indoors.

Growing

Papyruses grow well in **full sun to partial shade**. The soil should be a **wet, loamy** pond mix. They are often grown at the edges of the pond so the plant crowns are submerged in up to 15 cm (6") of water. Containers make it easier to move them to a sheltered location for winter.

Divide the plants as needed in spring when they begin to outgrow their containers. Plants can be grown indoors for the winter as long as the soil is kept consistently moist.

Tips

Grown for their foliage, papyruses make attractive additions to pond edges, bog gardens or in the moist soil next to the pond.

New plants can be propagated by floating, fresh-cut flowerheads with leaf whorls attached upside down on the water. Cut the stems an inch or two below the leafy whorl. New plants can be potted once the rootlets have formed.

Recommended

C. alternifolius (dwarf umbrella palm) grows 30–90 cm (12–36") tall and spreads about 40 cm (16"). It forms a tufted clump of upright stems topped by clusters of yellow-brown flowers. A whorl of narrow, grass-like leaves surrounds the base of each cluster. (Zones 7–8)

C. haspan (*C. profiler,* dwarf papyrus) grows 30–90 cm (12–36") tall and spreads 45–60 cm (18–24"). It forms a small clump of stems that bear rounded clusters of tiny, brown flowers in summer. (Zone 8)

P. haspan

C. longus (umbrella sedge, sweet galingale) grows 60 cm–1.5 m (2–5') tall and spreads 90 cm (36") or more. It forms a tufted clump of upright stems and bears clusters of small, reddish brown flowers in late summer and fall.

Problems & Pests

Rare problems with leaf spot, rust and smut can occur.

C. alternifolious

Parrot Feather

Myriophyllum

Habit: submerged or emergent aquatic oxygenating perennial
Height: 45 cm–1.5 m (18"–5') **Spread:** indefinite
Hardiness: zones 5–8

THESE LOVELY PLANTS with
feathery foliage are at home both in
the pond and next to it. They often
spread beneath the water and climb
up over the pond edges.

*A parrot feather's
submerged leaves
are soft, feathery
and yellow-green
in colour, whereas
the emergent leaves
are smaller, coarser,
less finely divided
and more of a blue-
green hue.*

Growing

Parrot feathers grow best in **full sun**. The soil should be a **wet, loamy** pond mix. They can be grown in containers or directly in the pond. The closer to the pond edge these plants are, the more likely they are to grow up onto the pond banks. Some water gardeners enjoy this effect, while others dislike it.

Divide your parrot feathers as required in spring or fall to control their spread or when the plants threaten to outgrow their containers. Cut the trailing stems back in summer if needed. In fall, cut the plants back so that they remain well below the ice, or move a section into an indoor aquarium for winter.

Tips

Although these plants are usually grown for their attractive submerged foliage, they often poke out of the water or even grow up the banks of a water feature.

These oxygenators can be planted 5–20 bunches per m^2 (1–2 bunches for every 1–2 ft^2) of water surface area. However, parrot feathers are not as efficient at consuming nutrients as many other oxygenating plants; depending on them as your only oxygenators can result in excessive algae growth.

Recommended

M. aquaticum (parrot feather, diamond milfoil) is a creeping plant with long, generally unbranched stems. Tiny, yellow flowers are produced underwater in summer.

M. aquaticum (above & below)

Problems & Pests

Parrot feathers rarely suffer from any problems, but young growth may be nibbled by fish.

Pennywort

Hydrocotyle

Habit: marginal or pondside perennial **Height:** 5–25 cm (2–10")
Spread: 40 cm (16") to indefinite **Hardiness:** zones 4–8

THESE PRETTY LITTLE groundcover
plants quickly fill in around the edges
of a pond, creating a low mass of
round, decorative foliage.

*A popular aquarium
plant,* H. verticillata
*can sometimes be
purchased at
aquarium supply
shops.*

Growing

Pennyworts grow well in **full sun to partial shade**. The soil should be a **wet, loamy** pond mix, in up to 5 cm (2") of water.

Divide the plants in spring, when they have outgrown their containers or to control their spread. Trim them back as needed. They can be moved indoors for winter, but they should be kept in moist soil in a bright location.

Tips

Pennyworts are popular groundcovers near streams and waterfalls, where the stems will trail in the moving water. They can be placed in the shallows, planted next to the pond or included in a bog garden. They are useful for filling in the spaces around other, taller plants.

Recommended

H. verticillata grows 10–25 cm (4–10") tall and spreads 40–90 cm (16–36") or more. In summer, this

H. vulgaris (above & below)

low, round-leaved, creeping plant bears small, white flowers. (Zones 5–8)

H. vulgaris grows 5–15 cm (2–6") tall and spreads indefinitely, with new roots developing along the stems as they spread. This low, round-leaved, creeping plant bears small, white, summer flowers tinged with pink.

Pennyworts rarely suffer from any problems.

Periwinkle
Myrtle
Vinca

Habit: pondside perennial **Height:** 10–20 cm (4–8") **Spread:** indefinite
Hardiness: zones 3–8

TRAILING PLANTS LIKE periwinkle make attractive additions to the edges of a water feature, where they can trail into the water and spread around larger plants.

Growing

Periwinkles grow well in **partial to full shade**. The soil should be of **average fertility** and **moist**—mulching helps keep it moist. These plants prefer a sheltered location.

Cut the plants back in early spring as needed to control their spread.

Tips

Periwinkles make attractive ground-covers on shady banks next to a pond, and they can also be grown at the edges of a bog garden. They are good transition plants for blending the pondside garden with other parts of the garden.

V. minor (above & below)

Recommended

V. minor (lesser periwinkle, creeping myrtle) forms a low, loose mat of trailing stems. Purple or blue flowers are borne in a main flush in spring and bloom sporadically throughout summer and fall. Many cultivars are available, including those with varie gated leaves and reddish purple or white flowers.

Problems & Pests

Rare problems with scale insects, leafhoppers, aphids and leaf spot can occur.

Periwinkles root along their stems as they spread. Rooted sections can be planted elsewhere in the garden or potted up and given as gifts to fellow gardeners.

Pickerel Weed

Pontederia

Habit: marginal aquatic perennial **Height:** 45–90 cm (18–36")
Spread: 60–90 cm (24–36") or more **Hardiness:** zones 4–8

EASTERN CANADIAN GARDENERS who also enjoy fishing will probably recognize these plants; pickerel weed is common in eastern ponds and lakes.

Growing

Pickerel weeds grow best in **full sun** but tolerate partial shade. The soil should be a **wet, loamy** pond mix, in up to 50 cm (20") of water.

Divide the plants as needed in spring when they have outgrown their containers or to control their spread.

Tips

Pickerel weeds are attractive plants to include in the margins of the pond or in a very wet bog garden. They help naturalize the setting, particularly within their native eastern North American range.

Recommended

P. cordata can spread indefinitely once established. It has upright shoots extending 45–90 cm (18–36") above the waterline and it produces spikes of blue or purple flowers all summer.

Problems & Pests

Rare problems with spider mites and rust can occur.

As the name suggests, pickerel weed in natural lakes and ponds often attracts pickerel or pike, so you may want to add these fish to your pond if space allows.

P. cordata (above & below)

Pitcher Plant

Sarracenia

Habit: carnivorous bog perennial **Height:** 5–90 cm (2–36")
Spread: 90 cm (up to 36") **Hardiness:** zones 2–8

PITCHER PLANT'S DECORATIVE leaves form long tubes and are often variegated with shades of red, white and pink. It's worth it to create a true bog garden just to be able to grow this stunning plant.

The common pitcher plant is the floral emblem of Newfoundland and Labrador.

S. purpurea (all photos)

Growing

Pitcher plants grow best in **full sun.** The soil should be **humus rich, acidic** and **wet,** with the waterline 10–15 cm (4–6") below the plant's crown. A mix of **peat** and **sphagnum moss** combined with **sand** is often used.

Division is required only if you want to propagate the plants. Carefully separate the crowns in mid-spring, avoid damage to the roots and replant the divisions immediately.

Tips

Pitcher plants are not considered easy to grow, but a water feature helps create the growing conditions they need. Both beautiful and unusual, they are popular additions to the bog garden, and their insect-eating tubes that rise mysteriously out of the damp ground are certain to be a conversation piece.

The tubes or pitchers are actually modified leaves. Hairs or spikes along the insides of the tubes allow insects to climb in but not out. Once an insect reaches the bottom of a tube, the plant digests it.

Recommended

S. leucophylla (*S. drummondii*, white trumpet, white-topped pitcher plant) has slender, green pitchers 25–90 cm (10–36") tall with purple-tinged, white tops and it spreads up to 90 cm (36"). Nodding, purple flowers are produced in spring. (Zones 6–8)

S. purpurea (common pitcher plant, huntsman's cup) bears purple-veined, green pitchers 5–50 cm (2–20") tall and spreads up to 90 cm (36"). Nodding flowers in dark purple, red or (rarely) yellow appear in spring.

Problems & Pests

Scale insects, mealybugs and aphids can cause problems.

Plume Poppy
Macleaya
Macleaya

Habit: pondside perennial **Height:** 1.8–3 m (6–10') **Spread:** 90 cm (36") or more **Hardiness:** zones 3–8

PLUME POPPY IS a bold and vigorous plant. In moist soil next to your pond it can even be invasive, but its fantastic foliage and airy flower clusters are worth any efforts required to control its spread.

Growing

Plume poppies prefer **full sun** but tolerate partial shade. The soil should be of **average fertility, humus rich** and **moist**. To restrict the growth of these plants you may prefer to grow them in large, sunken containers with the bottoms cut out.

Deadhead your plume poppies to keep them looking neat and to prevent excessive self-seeding. Divide them every two or three years in spring or fall to control their clump sizes.

M. cordata (above & below)

Tips

Best suited to large gardens and large water features, these dramatic plants make spectacular pondside specimens and create a quick, attractive privacy screen. Consider planting them on the far side of your pond and give them room to spread.

Recommended

M. cordata forms a tall, narrow clump with undulating, lobed leaves and plumes of creamy white flowers in mid- and late summer.

Problems & Pests

Slugs may attack young growth, and anthracnose can be a problem during warm, humid weather.

Plume poppies look quite different from other members of the poppy family.

Primrose
Cowslip
Primula

Habit: pondside perennial **Height:** 10–60 cm (4–24")
Spread: 20–60 cm (8–24") **Hardiness:** zones 4–8

PLANTED IN A group beside the pond, primroses will
provide an unparalleled burst of colour in spring.

P. x bullesiana *is
particularly attractive when
planted in groups and left to
naturalize.*

Growing

The primroses described here prefer **partial shade** but tolerate full sun if the soil stays moist. The soil should be **fertile, humus rich, neutral to acidic** and **moist**.

Division, which can be done in spring, isn't required very often.

Tips

With their bright flowers and long blooming periods, these plants are welcome additions to the pondside garden. Their fondness for moist soil makes them a good choice for a spot on the edge of a bog garden or next to a waterfall, where splashing water keeps the soil moist.

Recommended

P. x *bullesiana* (hybrid candelabra primrose) grows 45–60 cm (18–24") tall and spreads 25–60 cm (10–24"). It forms a basal rosette of leaves and a tall flower stalk with tiered rings of summer flowers in shades of yellow, orange, pink and purple.

P. bullesiana (above), *P. x polyanthus* (below)

P. x *polyanthus* (hybrid polyantha primrose) grows 10–20 cm (4–8") tall and spreads 20–45 cm (8–18"). It forms a basal rosette of evergreen leaves and bears clusters of red, orange, yellow, pink, purple or white flowers in spring and early summer. (Zones 5–8)

Problems & Pests

Occasional problems with slugs, snails, aphids, spider mites, root rot, rust and leaf spot are possible.

Ribbon Grass
Gardener's Garters
Phalaris

Habit: marginal or pondside evergreen perennial grass **Height:** 60 cm–1.5 m
(2–5') **Spread:** 90 cm (36") to indefinite **Hardiness:** zones 2–8

THIS BRIGHTLY STRIPED grass forms large, attractive
clumps that provide shelter for small animals. Visiting frogs
and mice will appreciate it.

*With their striking, striped leaves, ribbon
grass cultivars are among the most brightly
coloured grasses suitable for ponds.*

P. arundinacea 'Strawberries & Cream' (opposite page), *P. arundinacea* (above), *P. a.* var. *picta* (below)

Growing

Ribbon grasses grow well in **full sun to partial shade**. The soil should be of **average fertility** and **moist to wet,** in water up to 30 cm (12") deep. It is best to plant ribbon grasses in large containers to control their spread.

When they have outgrown their containers, divide ribbon grasses as needed in spring or early summer. Cut back the previous year's growth in spring.

Tips

These vigorous additions to a moist, pondside area or the margins of the pond provide interest in winter as well as shelter for wildlife.

Ribbon grasses can be invasive and difficult to remove once established. Planting them in sunken containers lets you to enjoy them without allowing them to take over the garden.

Recommended

P. arundinacea forms quick-spreading clumps of long, narrow, sometimes yellow-striped leaves. Cultivars with brightly striped foliage, in colours such as pink, cream and green, have been developed.

Problems & Pests

Occasional problems with rust, smut and leaf spot can occur.

Rodgersia
Rodgersia

Habit: pondside perennial **Height:** 90 cm–1.5 m (3–5')
Spread: 60–90 cm (24–36") **Hardiness:** zones 3–8

SHADE- AND MOISTURE-LOVING rodgersia quickly fills large spaces next to water features and provides a fast-growing privacy screen.

Rodgersia's flower clusters can be cut and dried for use in flower arrangements.

Growing

Rodgersias grow best in **partial to light shade** but tolerate full sun when the soil stays moist. The soil should be **fertile, humus rich** and **moist**. Excessive exposure can cause leaf scorch, so a location that provides protection from wind and hot afternoon sun is preferable.

Rodgersias rarely need dividing, but you can do so in spring to propagate more plants.

Tips

These bold plants give the waterside garden a dramatic appearance. Planted in moist soil near your pond, rodgersias create a strong focal point. When they are not in flower, their dark green leaves make a fine backdrop for other plants and flowers.

Recommended

R. aesculifolia (fingerleaf rodgersia) forms a clump of horsechestnut-like leaves. It produces clusters of tiny,

R. pinnata (above & below)

white or pink flowers on tall stalks in mid- or late summer.

R. pinnata (featherleaf rodgersia) grows 90 cm–1.2 m (3–4') tall, forming a clump of horsechestnut-like leaves. It bears large clusters of tiny, red, pink or off-white flowers in mid- and late summer. (Zones 4–8)

Problems & Pests

Slugs and snails may attack young foliage.

Rush
Corkscrew Rush
Juncus

Habit: marginal aquatic or bog garden perennial **Height:** 40–80 cm (16–32")
Spread: 60 cm (2') **Hardiness:** zones 4–8

THESE RUSHES ARE popular, eye-catching plants, particularly the curly- or spiral-leaved cultivars. They will fascinate gardeners and visitors alike.

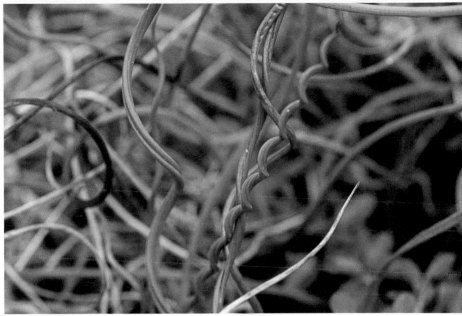

J. effusus 'Spiralis' (above & below)

Growing

Rushes grow well in **full sun to partial shade**. The soil should be a **wet, acidic, loamy** pond mix, in up to 10 cm (4") of water.

Divide rushes in spring or early summer to propagate more plants.

Tips

Plant rushes at the pond's edge or in a bog garden where they can easily be seen and approached, such as near a sitting area, pathway or bridge.

Recommended

J. effusus (soft rush) forms a tufted clump of long, flexible, stem-like leaves and bears insignificant flowers in summer. The naturally occurring species is rarely grown. **'Spiralis'** forms a tangled mass of curling and corkscrew-like leaves, and cultivars with more corkscrew-like leaves are becoming available. (Zones 6–8)

J. inflexus (hard rush) forms a clump of stiff, stem-like leaves 60–80 cm (24–32") tall. **'Afro'** has more tightly spiraled stems than 'Spiralis'.

Problems & Pests

Problems with fungal leaf spot, stem rot and rust are possible.

The curling stems of 'Spiralis' are popular in floral arrangements.

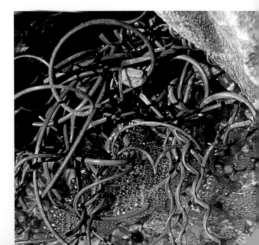

Salvinia

Floating Fern, Water Fern

Salvinia

Habit: floating aquatic tender perennial fern **Height:** 5–10 cm (2–4")
Spread: indefinite **Hardiness:** tender perennial

THESE PECULIAR-LOOKING, hairy-leaved, floating ferns spread
quickly over the water surface.

S. natans (all photos)

Growing

Salvinias grow best in **full sun**. They **float** on the water's surface and require no soil. They dislike moving water, so keep them in a **still** area of your pond.

To control their quick spread, thin these plants out regularly in summer and put them in your compost bin. Salvinias can be overwintered by removing a few plants in fall and keeping them in a brightly lit aquarium.

Tips

These unique-looking floating plants shade the water's surface and provide shelter for fish.

Recommended

S. natans forms short stems of floating leaves. The leaves are borne in threes, with two above the water and one longer, lacy, underwater leaf that functions like a root.

Unlike most terrestrial ferns, which have triangular, divided leaves, salvinias are unique floating ferns with soft, hairy, oval leaves.

Sedge

Carex

Habit: pondside, marginal aquatic or bog garden perennial
Height: 60 cm–1.4 m (24"–4½') **Spread:** 30 cm–1.2 m (12"–4')
Hardiness: zones 3–8

THESE GRASS-LIKE PLANTS, popular with ornamental grass afi-
cionados, grow exceptionally well in moist soil next to a water feature.

Sedges are among the most attractive grass-
like plants for the moist, pondside garden. In
the wild, their dense, tufted clumps can
mislead hikers into believing the ground is
more solid than it is.

Growing

Sedges grow well in **full sun to partial shade**. The soil should be **fertile** and **moist to wet,** in water up to 10 cm (4") deep.

When your sedge clumps outgrow their space or become overgrown, divide them in early summer. Old growth can be cut back or thinned by hand in spring to make way for the new growth.

Tips

Sedges make attractive grasses for the shallow margins of the pond. They can also be included in boggy areas.

Recommended

C. elata 'Aurea' (Bowles' golden sedge) grows 60–90 cm (24–36") tall and spreads about 45 cm (18"), forming a clump of arching, grass-like, yellow leaves with green edges. It bears spikes of tiny, brown or green flowers in early summer. (Zones 5–8)

C. pendula (drooping sedge, weeping sedge) forms a clump of graceful, arching, grass-like, green leaves.

Drooping spikes of brown flowers are borne on long stems in late spring and early summer. (Zones 5–8)

C. pseudocyperus (grey sedge, hop sedge) grows 60–100 cm (24–40") tall, with an equal spread, and forms a clump of grassy, bright green leaves. In early summer, contrasting dark green spikes of flowers appear.

Problems & Pests

Problems with aphids, fungal leaf spot, rust and smut can occur.

Shield Fern
Sword Fern, Holly Fern
Polystichum

Habit: evergreen pondside perennial fern **Height:** 30 cm–1.2 m (12"–4')
Spread: 20 cm–1.2 m (8"–4') **Hardiness:** zones 3–8

THESE EVERGREEN FERNS are a treat, providing greenery all year.
The fronds vary significantly from species to species; some contrast
and others complement each other.

*Christmas fern is a lower-growing
and less invasive hardy fern. The use
of its fronds as Christmas decorations
gave the plant its common name.*

Growing

Shield ferns grow well in **partial shade to full shade**. The soil should be **fertile, humus rich** and **moist**.

Divide these ferns in spring to propagate more plants or to control their spread. Dead and weary-looking fronds should be removed in spring, before the new ones fill in.

Tips

These ferns are a good choice for a shaded pondside garden. They can be included in a bog garden but are better suited to moist rather than wet conditions. In areas with little or no snow cover, you can enjoy the green fronds all winter.

Recommended

P. acrostichoides (Christmas fern) grows 30–45 cm (12–18") tall and spreads 30–90 cm (12–36"), forming a circular clump of arching, evergreen fronds. It is native to northeastern North America.

P. munitum (western sword fern) grows 60 cm–1.2 m (2–4') tall, with an equal spread, forming circular clusters of evergreen fronds. This West Coast native prefers cool, moist conditions and doesn't grow well in hot summer weather. (Zones 4–8)

P. setiferum (soft shield fern, hedge fern) spreads 45–90 cm (18–36"), forming an attractive circular mound of bright green, evergreen fronds. Some of the many cultivars that have been developed in Europe, including dwarf plants and cultivars with more finely divided leaflets, are occasionally available in Canada. (Zones 5–8)

P. acrostichoides

Shield ferns are usually free of problems.

P. munitum

Silver Grass
Zebra Grass
Miscanthus

Habit: pondside perennial grass **Height:** 1.5–4 m (5–13')
Spread: 90 cm–1.2 m (3–4') or more **Hardiness:** zones 3–8

BOTH THE FOLIAGE and flowers of these tall grasses are decorative and create a stunning display when they move in the wind.

Silver grass is relatively free of problems, and its stems remain standing through winter, providing interest and reminding you of summer.

Growing

Silver grass grows best in **full sun**. The soil should be of **average fertility, moist** and **well drained**. Giant silver grass tolerates wet soil and even standing water.

Once established, these grasses tend to spread rather vigorously, so they are often grown in sunken containers. Divide them as needed in spring when they have outgrown their containers or to control their spread. The stems and leaves can be left in place for winter, but they should be cut back in spring.

'Zebrinus' (opposite),
M. sinensis cultivars (above & below)

Tips

These tall grasses make good screening plants next to the pond; they will grow quickly and provide privacy for your sitting area. Although *M. sinensis* likes moist soil, it resents standing in water, especially in winter, so it shouldn't be planted in boggy areas.

Recommended

M. sacchariflorus 'Robustus' (giant silver grass) grows 1.5–2.1 m (5–7') tall. It forms a large clump of stiff stems with arching, green leaves, each with a silvery stripe running down the centre. The leaves turn red-orange in fall. The late-summer and fall flower plumes change from silvery to rusty as they mature.

M. sinensis (Japanese silver grass) can grow 1.8–4 m (6–13') tall, depending on the cultivar, and spreads 90 cm–1.2 m (3–4'). It forms a clump of upright stems and long, arching leaves. Loose, tan or grey flower clusters with purple tinges appear in fall. The many cultivars available include ones with variegated leaves, dwarf sizes and more attractive flower plumes. **'Zebrinus'** (zebra grass) is a popular cultivar with horizontal yellow stripes on its leaves. (Zones 4–8; some cultivars are less hardy)

Spearwort
Water Crowfoot, Buttercup
Ranunculus

Habit: submerged or marginal aquatic perennial **Height:** 10–70 cm (4–28") **Spread:** 75 cm (30") to indefinite **Hardiness:** zones 5–8

THESE PLANTS FORM a dense mat of foliage in the shallow margins of the pond, and they will be covered with cheerful flowers nearly all summer.

Growing

Spearworts grow well in **full sun to partial shade**. The soil should be a **wet, loamy** pond mix. *R. aquatilis* can be planted in 20–50 cm (8–20") of water, and *R. flammula* can be grown in up to 15 cm (6") of water.

Both of the plants recommended below grow best in containers because they tend to spread rampantly if unchecked. Divide them in spring or fall as needed when they have outgrown their containers or to control their spread.

Tips

Despite their vigorous growing tendencies, these plants, with their long blooming periods, are welcome in the margins of the pond, where they fill in quickly. They also enjoy moving water and can be planted alongside a stream. As a bonus, *R. flammula* consumes excess nutrients, thus helping to control algae spread while requiring less light than most oxygenating plants.

Recommended

R. aquatilis (water crowfoot) grows about 10 cm (4") above the water's surface and spreads indefinitely. Sometimes treated as an annual, this submerged or marginal aquatic perennial produces lacy, finely divided, submerged leaves as well as round or kidney-shaped, floating leaves. It bears abundant, yellow-centred, white flowers on the water's surface in mid-summer.

R. flammula (lesser spearwort) grows 20–70 cm (8–28") tall and spreads 75 cm (30") or more. This marginal

R. flammula (above & below)

aquatic perennial bears bright yellow flowers in summer.

Problems & Pests

Occasional problems with leaf spot, aphids, slugs and snails are possible.

R. aquatilis is generally grown as a submerged plant. If planted in a wet bog garden, it will develop only floating leaves.

Spike Rush
Hairgrass
Eleocharis

Habit: submerged oxygenating or marginal aquatic perennial **Height:** 15–45 cm (6–18") **Spread:** 20–30 cm (8–12") to indefinite **Hardiness:** zones 3–8

THE TWO PLANTS recommended below form attractive, grassy clumps either at the bottom of the pond or on the shallow margins.

*The Chinese water chestnut (*E. tuberosa, *formerly* E. dulcis)*, popular in Asian cooking, is also grown by some Canadian water gardeners.*

Growing

Both species grow well in **full sun to partial shade**. The soil should be a **wet, slightly acidic, loamy** pond mix. *E. acicularis* prefers about 30 cm (12") of water, and *E. montevidensis* can be grown in up to 10 cm (4") of water.

Growing these plants in containers helps restrict their spread, but they also propagate by self-seeding. Divide them in spring as needed when they outgrow their containers or to control their spread. Where it is not hardy, *E. acicularis* can be overwintered indoors in an aquarium.

E. montevidensis (above & below)

Both of the recommended species are generally free of problems.

Tips

E. acicularis is a vigorous competitor for pond nutrients and therefore keeps algae growth under control. It can survive in most Canadian ponds as long as it remains below the ice line in winter, and it may overwhelm other pond-bottom plants. Use 5–20 bunches of plants per m² (1–2 bunches for every 1–2 ft²) of water surface area.

E. montevidensis tolerates moving water, making it a good choice for both ponds and stream side.

Recommended

E. acicularis (hairgrass) grows 20–30 cm (8–12") tall, with an equal or greater spread. It is a submerged, clump-forming grass with narrow, bright green leaves. (Zones 5–8)

E. montevidensis (spike rush) grows 15–45 cm (6–18") tall and spreads indefinitely. This marginal aquatic forms a clump of stiff emergent stems.

Swamp Hibiscus
Rosemallow
Hibiscus

Habit: pondside or bog perennial **Height:** 90 cm–2.4 m (3–8')
Spread: 24–36" (60–90 cm) **Hardiness:** zones 4–8

QUITE POSSIBLY THE boldest flowering plant for your moist, pond-side garden, swamp hibiscus is sure to draw attention with its brightly coloured, dinner plate-sized flowers.

*The flower of a swamp hibiscus
can be up to 30 cm (12") across.*

Growing

Swamp hibiscuses prefer **full sun**. The soil should be **fertile, humus rich** and **moist**. The naturally occurring species can be planted in water up to 15 cm (6") deep, but many cultivars have been developed to tolerate ordinary garden culture and may not perform as well in standing water.

Divide these plants in spring on the rare occasions that they need reinvigorating or if you want to propagate them. Deadheading keeps them looking tidy.

Tips

With their bold flowers, swamp hibiscuses make quite a statement in late summer. Include them in your bog garden or pondside garden. They will thrive in an area that periodically floods.

These plants die back completely in fall and are slow to emerge in spring; be sure to mark their location so you don't accidentally dig them up or damage them in the spring.

Recommended

H. moscheutos is a large, vigorous plant with strong stems that bear enormous red, pink or white flowers from mid-summer to frost. Dwarf cultivars and cultivars selected for flower colour are available.

Dwarf cultivars such as **'Disco'** and cultivars selected for flower colour, such as **'Lady Baltimore'** with pink flowers and **'Lord Baltimore'** with red flowers, are available.

H. moscheutos cultivars (above & below)

Problems & Pests

Problems with rust, fungal leaf spot, bacterial blight, *Verticillium* wilt, rot, aphids, whiteflies, mites and caterpillars are possible.

Sweet Flag
Japanese Rush
Acorus

Habit: marginal aquatic perennial **Height:** 10 cm–1.5 m (4"–5')
Spread: 10–60 cm (4–24") **Hardiness:** zones 4–8

SWEET FLAG IS ONE of the most popular marginal plants. With its glossy, often striped leaves, it creates an attractive stand along pond edges—the kind of sheltered location frogs and fish enjoy.

A. calamus was a popular moat-side plant in the past.

Growing

Sweet flag grows best in **full sun**. The soil should be a **wet, loamy** pond mix. *A. calamus* can be grown in water up to 20 cm (8") deep, and *A. graminus* can be grown in water up to 5 cm (2") deep.

Both species can be grown in containers or planted directly in the pond. They rarely need dividing, and *A. graminus* dislikes having its roots disturbed.

Tips

These plants are much admired for their habits as well as for the wonderful spicy fragrance of their crushed leaves. Include them at the margins of your pond or in the permanently moist soil of a bog garden.

Recommended

A. calamus (sweet flag) grows from 60 cm– 1.5 m (2–5') tall and spreads about 60 cm (2'). This large, clump-forming plant has fragrant, long, narrow, bright green foliage. **'Variegatus'** is a popular and commonly available cultivar with yellow, cream and green on its vertically striped leaves.

A. graminius (Japanese rush, dwarf sweet flag) grows 10–30 cm (4–12") tall, with an equal spread. This smaller plant forms fan-shaped clumps of fragrant, glossy green, long, narrow leaves. Even smaller cultivars are available, as well as ones with variegated leaves. (Zones 5–8)

Problems & Pests

Root rot, leaf spot and rust can occasionally cause problems.

A. calamus (above), *A. graminius* cultivar (below)

Thalia
Hardy Canna
Thalia

Habit: marginal aquatic **Height:** 2–3 m (6½–10') **Spread:** 2–3 m (6½–10')
Hardiness: zones 5–8 or tender perennial

THALIAS WILL GIVE your pond a tropical appearance. Grow them in the middle of the pond if it is large enough; thalia leaves stand out above the water and provide an accent for your water lilies floating below.

Growing

Thalias grow best in **full sun**. The soil should be a **wet, loamy** pond mix, with 15–30 cm (6–12") of water for *T. dealbata* and up to 15 cm (6") of water for *T. geniculata* forma *ruminoides*.

Divide the plants as needed in spring when they have outgrown their space or their containers.

Tips

Plant them in the shallow water at the edge. Consider growing the tender *T. geniculata* forma *ruminoides* in a container so you can easily bring it indoors for winter and treat it as a tropical houseplant.

Strong winds can blow these plants over. It is best to grow them in a sheltered location.

Recommended

T. dealbata (powdery thalia) forms a clump of leaf stalks with large leaves. A powdery white coating gives the leaves a grey-green colour. This plant bears purple flowers in summer. (Zones 5–8)

T. geniculata forma *ruminoides* (red-stemmed thalia) is very similar to powdery thalia, but it has red or purple leaf stems and isn't as hardy. (Grown as a tender perennial.)

With its long leaf stalks and long-stemmed flower spikes, the rarely troubled thalia has a graceful and exotic appearance. Both species recommended above can be overwintered indoors where they aren't hardy.

T. dealbata (above & below)

Turtle Head
Shell Flower
Chelone

Habit: pondside or bog garden perennial **Height:** 45–90 cm (18–36")
Spread: 45–60 cm (18–24") **Hardiness:** zones 3–8

TURTLE HEAD'S DARK green foliage and bright pink flowers make
this plant worth growing alone, but it also contrasts beautifully with
other pondside perennials.

Growing

Turtle heads grow well in **full sun to partial shade**. The soil should be **fertile, humus rich** and **moist to wet**.

Divide these plants as needed in spring or fall.

These plants can tolerate a heavy clay soil.

C. obliqua (all photos)

Tips

Late-season blooms appear just as most other plants start to fade, making the attractive turtle head a welcome addition to moist, pond-side plantings or bog gardens.

These plants are also useful in areas that flood periodically.

The flowers of turtle head are weather tolerant, and they suffer no damage from heavy rains.

Recommended

C. obliqua is an upright plant that forms a dense mound of foliage. It bears pink or purple flowers in late summer through mid-fall. A cultivar with white flowers is also available.

Problems & Pests

Problems with powdery mildew, leaf spot, rust, slugs and snails are possible.

Most turtle head species are native wildflowers in the eastern or southern parts of North America.

Umbrella Plant

Darmera

Habit: pondside or bog garden plant **Height:** 90 cm–1.2 m (3–4')
Spread: 36" (90 cm) or more **Hardiness:** zones 5–8

THIS BOLD PLANT provides interest for the entire growing season. It
flowers in spring before the leaves emerge, and the large, prominently
veined leaves form a dark green clump in summer that turns red in fall.

D. peltata (above & below)

Growing

Umbrella plants grow well in **sun to partial shade**. The soil should be a **moist to wet, loamy** pond mix.

Slow-growing umbrella plants probably won't need dividing very often, but you can do so in spring to propagate more plants.

Tips

Include umbrella plants in a bog garden or wet area around your pond. They create quite a conversation piece in spring when the flower stalks, which can grow up to 2 m (6½') tall, emerge before the leaves.

Recommended

D. peltata forms a clump of long stems topped by large, round leaves. It bears rounded clusters of pink flowers in late spring.

Umbrella plants somewhat resemble gunneras, but they are two zones hardier and they rarely suffer from any problems.

Valerian
Garden Heliotrope
Valeriana

Habit: pondside perennial **Height:** 1–2 m (3½–6½') **Spread:** 40–80 cm (16–32") **Hardiness:** zones 2–8

VALERIAN IS KNOWN to many as a herbal remedy for insomnia, but it deserves to be well known as a fragrant, long-blooming addition to your moist, pondside plantings.

Growing

Valerians grow well in **full sun to light shade**. The soil should be of **average fertility** and **moist**.

Divide the plant clumps in spring or fall to rejuvenate them or for propagation.

Tips

These attractive and fragrant plants do well in moist, pondside plantings. In a bog garden, they should be kept on the edges because they like moist but not soggy conditions.

Recommended

V. officinalis, an upright plant with lacy foliage, bears clusters of fragrant, white or pink flowers in summer.

Problems & Pests

Occasional problems with leaf spot and powdery mildew can occur.

V. officinalis (above & below)

The dried roots of V. officinalis *are used to make a tea that helps people fall asleep.*

Virginia Bluebells
Virginia Cowslip
Mertensia

Habit: pondside perennial **Height:** 45–60 cm (18–24") **Spread:** 25–30 cm (10–12") **Hardiness:** zones 3–8

THESE PRETTY LITTLE plants are at home in a moist woodland and will provide a beautiful display of blue flowers in a shaded planting alongside your pond or stream. Virginia bluebells contrast nicely with the bright yellow flowers of marsh marigold, and they go dormant around the same time.

M. virginica (above & below)

Growing

Virginia bluebells grow well in **light to full shade**. The soil should be **fertile, humus rich** and consistently **moist**. They resent standing in water, however.

To propagate these plants, divide them in early spring when new growth begins to emerge, taking care not to disturb the roots too much.

Tips

For a striking colour display in spring, pair Virginia bluebells with marsh marigolds. Virginia bluebells are also good companions for summer bloomers that bush out as the bluebells begin to die back.

Recommended

M. virginica (*M. pulmonarioides*) is a clump-forming woodland perennial.

It bears clusters of blue flowers in mid-spring and usually goes dormant by mid-summer.

Problems & Pests

Occasional problems with slugs, snails, powdery mildew and rust can occur.

Don't forget about the Virginia bluebells in your garden; you might dig them up accidentally when they are dormant.

Water Forget-Me-Not

Myosotis

Habit: marginal aquatic perennial **Height:** 15–30 cm (6–12")
Spread: 30 cm (12") or more **Hardiness:** zones 3–8

BLOOMING ALMOST ALL spring and into early summer, these sun-loving plants provide colourful companionship for all your spring-blooming plants and herald the warmer days of summer.

Water forget-me-nots form a welcome groundcover in and around a water feature; they fill the spaces between other plants without overwhelming them.

Growing

Water forget-me-nots prefer **partial shade** but tolerate full sun. The soil should be of **average to poor fertility** and **moist to wet,** in water up to 10 cm (4") deep.

These often short-lived plants are unlikely to need dividing. They self-seed, and after a few years, they are likely to pop up here and there around your pond.

Tips

M. scorpioides (above & below)

Water forget-me-nots can be grown in containers and sunk at the edge of your pond, but many gardeners allow them to establish and self-seed in muddy soil directly in the pond. Learn to recognize the young seedlings so you don't accidentally pull them up when they first sprout.

Recommended

M. scorpioides (*M. palustris*) is a low, creeping, spreading plant. In early summer, it bears small clusters of blue flowers with centres of white, yellow or pink. Cultivars are available with darker blue or white flowers, or with more compact habits.

Cultivars are available with darker blue flowers (**'Sapphire'**), white flowers (**'Alba'**) or a more compact habit (**'Mermaid'**).

Problems & Pests

Problems with slugs, snails, mildew and mould can occur.

Water Hyacinth

Eichhornia

Habit: submerged or floating aquatic perennial **Height:** 10–45 cm (4–18")
Spread: 45 cm (18") or more **Hardiness:** tender perennial

WATER HYACINTHS ARE beautiful and interesting plants. They
shade the water's surface, and the dangling roots of *E. crassipes*
hyacinth provide a protected location for fish eggs and young fish.

Growing

Water hyacinths grow best in **full sun**. The soil for *E. azurea* should be a **wet, loamy** pond mix; *E. crassipes* should be allowed to **float** on the water's surface.

Scoop out excess plants as they multiply. These plants are not hardy and must be overwintered in containers of moist to wet soil in a bright, cool location indoors. Or you can buy new ones each spring.

Tips

Both species of water hyacinth recommended below reduce algae bloom by consuming excess nutrients in the water. The flowers, a lovely and desirable bonus, are not always as forthcoming as we might like.

Plants that grow prolifically but fail to flower probably need more nutrients. To avoid disturbing the nutrient balance of your pond, move a few plants to another container and feed them there before transferring them back to your pond. Continue cycling plants back and forth so you always have a few in bloom.

Recommended

E. azurea (blue water hyacinth) grows 10–15 cm (4–6") above the water's surface and spreads 45 cm (18") or more. This submerged plant produces narrow underwater leaves and floating rosettes of rounded or heart-shaped leaves. Spikes of light blue flowers with dark purple throats appear in summer.

E. crassipes (water hyacinth) grows about 45 cm (18") tall with an equal spread. It forms a floating rosette of

E. crassipes (above & below)

round leaves. A swollen, bulb-like structure at the base of each leaf helps the plant float. Fibrous roots trail in the water or sometimes root in the shallows of the pond. Late summer brings spikes of pale blue or pale purple flowers.

Water Lettuce

Pistia

Habit: floating aquatic perennial **Height:** up to 15 cm (6") **Spread:** indefinite
Hardiness: tender perennial

THOUGH HUMANS PROBABLY wouldn't enjoy a salad made of water lettuce, many of our fishy friends love nibbling on these interesting floating plants.

Water lettuces rarely suffer any problems. Despite their name and appearance, they are not edible.

Growing

Water lettuces grow best in **full sun** but tolerate some afternoon shade. The plants **float** on the water's surface and don't need soil. They spread by sending out runners with new plantlets at the ends.

Remove your water lettuces from the pond in fall; the leaves rot quickly after being damaged by frost. These plants can be overwintered in a warm, bright aquarium indoors, but it is often easier to purchase new ones each spring.

Tips

Water lettuces work best floating in the shallows of your pond. They produce a mat of bright green leaves that shades the water's surface, and the dangling roots provide food and shelter for young fish.

P. stratiotes with fairy moss and salvinia (above)

Recommended

P. stratiotes forms rosettes of rounded or triangular leaves that look like floating heads of cabbage or lettuce. Insignificant flowers appear in summer.

Water Lily
Nymphaea

Habit: submerged aquatic perennial with floating leaves **Height:** not applicable
Spread: 90 cm–3 m (3–10′) **Hardiness:** zones 4–8 or tender perennial

ADMIRED FOR THEIR attractive leaves as much as for their beautiful flowers, water lilies are among the most popular plants for water gardens. With the variety of plant sizes and flower colours available, there is a place in every pond for at least one of these beauties.

Growing

Water lilies grow best in **full sun**. The soil should be a **wet, loamy** pond mix. Most water lilies grow best in water about 60 cm (24") deep, but dwarf water lilies prefer 30 cm (12") of water.

These vigorous growers can be planted directly in the pond, but since their strong roots are capable of puncturing pond liners, many people grow them in containers. Plant a water lily at one side of its container, with the cut, non-growing end placed against the edge, and the growing end left to spread across the width of the container.

A newly planted water lily must be gradually lowered to its mature depth or else its buoyancy can cause the plant to uproot itself. Use blocks to temporarily raise the container closer to the water's surface, so that the crowns are about 5–10 cm (2–4") below the waterline. As the leaves emerge, gradually lower the container

'Colorado' (above), 'Steven Stravun' (below)

(this can require two or more people if it is large and heavy). The natural buoyancy of the leaves pulls on the rhizome and triggers a lengthening of the stem until the leaves are floating on the surface of the pond.

These heavy feeders need to be fertilized regularly during the growing season. Slow-release fertilizer tablets developed for water garden plants can be pushed into the soil at the edges of the container.

'Almost Black'

A jelly-like substance on the underside of a water lily's leaves is nothing to worry about. It's there to help the leaves stay afloat.

'Colorata'

Deadhead spent flowers and remove leaves that have begun to yellow. When the plant matures and the dense leaves begin to grow in, sometimes one on top of another, plan to divide the clump early in summer or the following spring.

Wait until water lilies completely die back before moving or cutting them back for the winter. Because of their high water content, they require a heavy frost to trigger dormancy.

Tips

Water lilies are among the most popular pond plants. They come in many sizes and are considered the pond's 'central' or 'structure' plants. As well as being decorative, they cast shade that reduces algae growth.

Tropical water lilies should be planted out only once the water temperature remains steady at about 21° C (70° F); colder water can stunt their growth. In Canada, they must be overwintered indoors. Move them to a very bright, cool location or a cool greenhouse during the winter (be sure to keep them wet). Or pull the tubers out of the pots after one or two frosts have killed the foliage. Cut the leaf stems and roots back to the tubers and remove all the soil. Separate small tubers from each plant's main tuber and let them all dry for a few days. Store them in airtight bags of damp peat moss in a cool, dark place such as a refrigerator set to 10–12° C (50–55° F). About a month before you return them to the pond, pot the plants up and set them in shallow water.

Recommended

N. **species** and **hybrids** are divided into two groups: hardy and tropical.

Hardy water lilies are submerged plants with round or heart-shaped, floating leaves. The showy summer flowers, which are generally two-thirds the size of the leaves, float among them. They open during the day in shades of pink, red, yellow, orange and white. Many species, hybrids and cultivars are available. Your local garden centre likely carries the plants that will do best in your region.

Tropical water lilies are submerged plants with round or heart-shaped, floating leaves, sometimes with toothed edges. Summer-blooming flowers are held above the water's surface. Day-blooming flowers open from late morning to late afternoon. Night-blooming flowers normally open in late afternoon and close by late morning the following day, but they may stay open longer during the cooler days of late summer and early fall. The flowers usually come in shades of pink, red, yellow and white, but blue-flowering varieties are especially prized. Check with your local garden centre to see what is available, or order by mail if you can't find what you want locally.

Problems & Pests

Insects and diseases that can disfigure the leaves include brown China-mark moths, water lily beetles, water lily aphids, false leaf-mining midges, snails, crown rot and fungal leaf spot. If an insect tears a young leaf while it's still curled up, long, jagged tears will remain once that leaf unfurls.

'Pygmy Hevola'

Wild water lilies are often "harvested" by amateur gardeners looking for cheap plants. This is not recommended; wild lilies can bring diseases, pests and leeches to the pond and it may take them up to three seasons to adapt to the backyard pond conditions.

N. alba

Water Poppy
Hydrocleys

Habit: submerged perennial with floating leaves   **Height:** not applicable
Spread: indefinite   **Hardiness:** tender perennial

REMINISCENT OF WATER LILY, this plant has small, round leaves and delicate-looking, cup-shaped, yellow flowers. Water gardeners with very little space may want to consider this plant if they haven't got room for the more vigorous water lilies.

Growing

Water poppies grow best in **full sun**. The soil should be a **wet, acidic, loamy** pond mix, in 15–30 cm (6–12") of water. These plants are best suited to areas with consistently warm summers because they tend to go dormant when the temperature regularly drops below 18° C (65° F).

Water poppies can be overwintered indoors as houseplants in very wet soil, but they require 10 hours of bright light per day to prevent new growth from being weak and lanky. Artificial lights are recommended.

Tips

Water poppies can be grown any-where in the pond, as long as they are in containers raised to the correct depth if they are in deep water.

If you plan to overwinter your water poppies indoors, bring them in before temperatures drop low enough to make them go dormant, which may be as early as late summer.

Recommended

H. nymphoides forms a clump of long stems that end at the water's sur-face with heart-shaped or round leaves. Yellow, poppy-like flowers with purple centres are held just above the water's surface in summer.

Water poppies are relatively free of problems. In winter, they can be grown in indoor hanging baskets, but be sure you keep the soil moist and provide artificial light during short winter days.

Watercress

Nasturtium

Habit: marginal aquatic perennial **Height:** 10–45 cm (4–18")
Spread: indefinite **Hardiness:** zones 4–8

A DENSE, SPREADING plant, watercress is often planted next to
streams and alongside waterfalls, where it fills in the edges of the
water feature and even trails into the water.

Growing

Watercress grows best in **full sun** but tolerates light to partial shade. The soil should be a **fertile, wet, loamy** pond mix, in water up to 10 cm (4") deep. It can be planted directly in the pond or grown in a container and sunk into the pond.

These plants rarely need dividing. Small pieces may break off and take root elsewhere—they can be removed or left to grow where they land.

Tips

Watercress enjoys both still and slow-moving water. Try planting it along the edges of streams and in the shallow margins of a pond.

For gardeners who enjoy adding watercress leaves to salads and sandwiches, these plants can be grown on a sunny window ledge in a tray or pot of wet soil.

Recommended

N. officinale is a low, spreading or trailing plant that produces small, white flowers from spring to fall.

Watercress rarely suffers from any problems. Its pungent, peppery-tasting leaves are a popular addition to salads and sandwiches.

Willow

Salix

Habit: pondside shrub **Height:** 1–4.5 m (3½–15') **Spread:** 1–4.5 m (3½–15')
Hardiness: zones 2–8

PLANT A BEAUTIFUL shrubby willow selection next to a
pond where its attractive habit and decorative stems and
foliage can create a striking display, often providing
interest all year.

Growing

Willows grow best in **full sun**. The soil should be of **average fertility** and **moist** but **well drained**.

S. alba 'Flame' should be cut back hard every few years to encourage the colourful young stems. The other two species mentioned below only need their awkward growth removed in early spring to keep them looking tidy. Remove damaged or dead growth as needed.

Tips

Large and weeping willows look beautiful near large water features, but in their aggressive search for water, they can damage the liners in small water gardens. The smaller willows listed below make attractive additions to the pondside garden, providing shade and shelter for pondside plants, as well as for you.

Recommended

S. alba **'Flame'** is a large shrub about 4.5 m (15') tall and wide, with young, dark red stems.

S. elaeagnos (rosemary willow) grows about 3.6 m (12') tall, with an equal spread. This delicate, arching shrub shows off the white undersides of its narrow, green leaves in a breeze. (Zones 4–7)

S. **'Hakuro Nishiki'** (*S. integra,* 'Alba Maculata') is a small shrub with long, arching or trailing branches. It grows 1–1.5 m (3½–5') tall and wide and has pink and white mottling on its green leaves. (Zones 5–8)

Problems & Pests

Crown gall, blight, leaf spot, rust, canker, powdery mildew, borers,

S. elaeagnos (above), *S.* 'Hakuro Nishiki' (below)

aphids and scale insects can cause trouble, often disfiguring a willow but not killing it.

Keep a close eye on the roots of willows to be sure that they aren't attempting forays through your pond liner. When you clean out your pond in spring, check the liner alongside the willow for bulges or spots that look as if they are being poked from beneath the liner. To avoid this potential problem from the outset, construct and install a root barrier of solid plastic or metal before you plant your willow.

Wood Rush

Luzula

Habit: evergreen pondside perennial **Height:** 30–80 cm (12–32")
Spread: 30–45 cm (12–18") **Hardiness:** zones 4–8

WOOD RUSH IS AN attractive grass-like plant, useful for softening the edges of your pond and providing winter interest.

L. nivea (all photos)

Growing

Woodrush grows well in **full to partial shade**, and it tolerates full sun if it has consistently moist soil. The soil should be of **average fertility, humus rich, moist** and **well drained**.

Divide the clumps in spring to propagate more plants or to encourage vigorous growth in plants with diminished growth.

Tips

Wood rushes are attractive groundcovers for the moist soil around your pond. *L. sylvatica* even tolerates periodic dry spells if grown in the shade, making it a good choice for a spot near your pond overflow, where moisture levels can vary greatly during the growing season.

Recommended

L. nivea (snowy wood rush) grows about 60 cm (2') tall, forming loose clumps of arching, grass-like leaves. It bears clusters of white flowers from early to mid-summer.

L. sylvatica (greater wood rush) forms a dense clump of grassy, dark green leaves. It bears small clusters of brown flowers in spring and early summer. Cultivars with yellow or variegated foliage are also available. (Zones 5–8)

Problems & Pests

Occasional problems with leaf spot and rust can occur.

Yellow Pond Lily
Spatterdock
Nuphar

Habit: submerged aquatic perennial with floating leaves
Height: not applicable **Spread:** indefinite **Hardiness:** zones 3–8

THE LARGE LEAVES and yellow flowers of *N. advena* and *N. lutea* make for impressive displays, but these large plants are best suited to large water features, and they take up far more space than a smaller home pond can provide.

Growing

N. advena and *N. lutea* grow best in **full sun**. They should be planted in a **wet, loamy** pond mix soil, in **cool** water 60 cm–2 m (2–6½') deep.

Be prepared to divide these fast-growing plants frequently to keep them blooming. Divide them every year or two if you're growing them in containers and less often if they are growing directly in the pond.

Tips

These plants are best suited to large water features because they require deeper water than is available in many home ponds. They also spread faster and wider than most small ponds can accommodate.

Recommended

N. advena (common spatterdock) forms a clump of long stems topped by large, round leaves that float on the water's surface. Yellow flowers tinged with red are held just above the surface in summer.

N. lutea (all photos)

N. lutea (yellow pond lily, yellow water lily, spatterdock) forms a clump of submerged stems and floating leaves that are larger than those of *N. advena*. Yellow flowers are held at or above the water's surface in summer. (Zones 4–8)

Problems & Pests

Leaf spot and smut are possible problems.

The above recommended species are good alternatives for large water features with temperatures too cool for water lilies.

Other Plants to Consider

Brooklime
Veronica beccabunga

These plants are excellent groundcovers for pond margins and bog gardens.

Brooklimes grow best in **full sun** in a **loamy** pond soil. Plant the crowns 10–20 cm (4–8") under water. Divide in summer after the first flush of flowers when your brooklimes outgrow their containers or to control their spread.

This low, spreading, marginal bog or pondside perennial bears loose spikes of blue flowers all summer. It grows 10–20 cm (4–8") tall and can spread indefinitely. Several cultivars are available. (Zones 4–8)

Butterwort
Pinguicula grandiflora

Butterworts make good additions to the bog garden or the moist soil around the edge of the pond, although they can be tricky to grow.

Butterworts grow well in **full sun to partial shade** in **sandy** or **peaty, acidic, moist** soil. These plants develop very few and very shallow roots and can easily be disturbed. They may require some winter protection to prevent them from being knocked about by animals, birds or people. Division, which is rarely required, can be done in early spring.

There are many butterwort species, but only a few are hardy in Canada.

This low-growing bog perennial forms a basal rosette of foliage with a stalk that holds purple, pink or white flowers in spring and early summer. The plant grows 15 cm (6") tall and spreads 10 cm (4"). Cool summers suit this plant best. A sticky fluid excreted from the leaves traps and digests small insects such as aphids, mosquitoes, whiteflies and fungus gnats. Grown successfully, butterworts can help control these common insect pests. (Zones 3–5 and to Zone 7 on the West Coast)

Cape Pondweed
Aponogeton distachyos

These attractive, fragrant-flowered plants can be planted at any depth in the average home pond, but the closer they are to the edge, the more you will enjoy the flowers' fragrance.

Butterwort

Cape pondweeds prefer **full sun** but tolerate partial shade with fewer flowers. The soil should be a **wet, loamy** pond mix. These plants prefer to be planted in water 30–90 cm (12–36") deep, either in containers or directly in the pond. Divide cape pondweeds in early spring or mid-summer when they have outgrown their containers or to control their spread if they were planted directly in the pond. Where they are not hardy, these plants can be overwintered indoors, and they may survive in colder zones if the rootzone remains below the ice in winter.

This submerged perennial has floating leaves and stems that grow long enough for the oblong leaves to float on the water's surface. The fragrant, white flowers bloom in spring and sometimes again in fall, on spikes that grow about 10 cm (4") out of the water. Plants can spread up to 100 cm (40"). (Zones 6–8)

Cape pondweed

Curly Water Thyme

Lagarosiphon major

These attractive plants avidly consume excess nutrients, easily outcompeting the algae.

Curly water thymes grow best in **full sun** in a **wet, loamy** pond mix. Plant 5–20 bunches per m² (1–2 bunches for every 1–2 ft²) of water surface area. These plants prefer still water, so avoid planting them near a waterfall or fountain. To control their spread in Zone 8, plant them in containers; in colder parts of Canada, they are likely to live only one growing season.

This submerged aquatic perennial, previously called *Elodea crispa*, has long, trailing, leafy stems that can spread indefinitely. The leaves curl back toward the stems, giving a snaky appearance. Small, white or pink flowers are borne in summer. (Zone 8)

During the growing season, cut these plants back as needed. Where the plants are hardy, simply cut them back hard in fall. Where they are not hardy, take cuttings and grow them in an aquarium over winter so you'll have plants for the following season. Pull out the parent plants in fall to prevent them from rotting in the pond during winter.

Hornwort

Ceratophyllum demersum

Hornworts compete with algae for nutrients and give the bottom of your pond a soft, feathery appearance.

Hornworts prefer **full sun** but tolerate partial shade. They may float freely in the water or grow anchored in mud or gravel, in water 60–90 cm (24–36") deep. Use 5–20 bunches per m^2 (1–2 bunches for every 1–2 ft^2) of water surface area. Overwintering buds break off in fall and sink to the bottom of the pond, after which the old plants can be removed. These plants generally survive in unfrozen water in colder-than-recommended zones, but if you are concerned that they won't be hardy in your pond, the overwintering buds can be moved to an indoor aquarium for winter.

This submerged oxygenating perennial can spread indefinitely, but it usually spreads only about 60 cm (2') before autumn puts an end to the growing season. The trailing stems have feathery foliage and bear inconspicuous flowers along their lengths in summer. (Zones 6–8)

Many popular pond fish use hornworts for spawning and enjoy its shade and shelter.

Hornwort

Pondweed

Marsh Cinquefoil
Potentilla palustris

Marsh cinquefoil looks at home in a natural pond or bog garden, especially combined with other native plants such as pickerel weed and narrow-leaved cattails. In fact, cinquefoils almost look like wildflowers among typically exotic and tropical-looking water garden plants.

Marsh cinquefoils grow best in **full sun** but tolerate partial shade. The soil should be a **moist to wet, loamy** pond mix, in water up to 10 cm (4") deep. These somewhat woody perennials rarely need dividing and can be propagated through stem cuttings.

This marginal aquatic or pondside perennial, known botanically as *Comarum palustre*, is an upright to sprawling plant with stems that often flop over when they reach a certain height. It grows 10–50 cm (4–20") tall and spreads 80 cm (32") or more. Red or purple flowers bloom in early summer. (Zones 3–8)

Pondweed
Canadian Pondweed, Canadian Waterpest
Elodea canadensis

These plants consume excess nutrients that would otherwise encourage algae growth. Small fish enjoy hiding among pondweed's leafy stems.

Pondweeds grow well in **full sun**. The soil should be a **wet, loamy** pond mix. Plant 5–20 bunches per m² (1–2 bunches per 1–2 ft²) of water surface area, either in containers or directly in the pond. Divide the plants in spring or fall as needed, when they have outgrown their containers or to control their spread. Trim them back as required during the growing season and cut them back to below the expected ice level in fall. Where they are not hardy, take cuttings in summer and grow them in an aquarium over winter.

This submerged oxygenating aquatic perennial has long, trailing, leafy stems that break easily. Stems can grow 3–4 m (10–13') tall and plants spread indefinitely. Small, purple-green flowers appear along the stems in summer. (Zones 5–8)

Starwort
Callitriche species

Starworts are excellent submerged oxygenators, but they can also be floating or marginal perennials. *C. verna's* floating rosettes of leaves add interest at the water's surface.

Starworts grow well in **full sun to partial shade** with **wet, loamy** soil. These plants can be grown directly in the pond or in containers. *C. hermaphroditica* does best when planted in water 45–60 cm (18–24") deep. *C. palustris* should be planted 5–20 cm (2–8") below the water's surface and can survive as a marginal plant in muddy, wet soil at the water's edge. Divide in spring or fall as often as needed to control their spread.

C. hermaphroditica (*C. autumnalis,* autumn starwort) grows about 50 cm (20") tall. This submerged plant has narrow leaves and does not produce floating rosettes. It bears small, inconspicuous, white flowers underwater in mid- to late summer. (Zones 5–8)

C. verna (*C. palustris,* water starwort) spreads 20–60 cm (8–24") and forms rosettes of foliage that float on the water's surface. It bears small, white flowers all summer. (Zones 4–8)

Starworts rarely suffer from any problems. In herbal medicine, they are used as diuretics and to treat some bladder and kidney disorders.

Tape grass

Tape Grass
Vallisneria species

This submerged oxygenating perennial or annual has long leaves that will float and trail across the water surface in a pond not quite deep enough to fully accommodate its length.

Tape grass grows well in **full sun to partial shade**. Soil is not necessary, but it can be planted in coarse **sand** or **gravel** to hold it in place, in water 30–90 cm (12–36") deep. Plant 5–20 bunches per m^2 (1–2 bunches for every 1–2 ft^2) of water surface area.

In fall, cut your tape grass back to well below the usual ice depth. If you expect your entire pond to freeze over in winter, or if tape grass has previously failed to overwinter in your pond, remove some of the small plantlets in late summer and grow them in a well-lit indoor aquarium for the winter. Otherwise, purchase new plants each spring.

V. americana (giant tape grass) forms a clump of narrow, ribbon-like leaves that grow 90 cm (36") or more in length. Too large for a small pond, it can be included in larger ponds and water features. (Zone 8)

V. spiralis (spiral tape grass) is a smaller plant that forms a clump of narrow, ribbon-like leaves that grow 20–90 cm (8–36") long. Flowers are produced on long, thin, spiral stems. This species is more useful in a home water feature because it isn't as large and doesn't grow as vigorously as giant tape grass. (Zone 8)

Water Soldier

Stratiotes species

These unusual plants are fun and interesting additions to the water garden. Purchased plantlets can be tossed into the pond in early summer. They will sink until they are ready to flower.

Water soldiers grow well in **full sun to partial shade**. These plants prefer to **float** in **slow-moving to still, slightly alkaline** water 30–60 cm (12–24") deep. Remove excess plants as needed to control their spread. When water soldiers begin to sink after flowering, they produce lots of overwintering buds. Where the plants aren't hardy, you can remove these buds and store them over winter in containers of mud and water in a cold but frost-free location indoors.

This submerged and periodically floating aquatic perennial grows 50 cm (20") tall and can spread indefinitely. It forms rosettes of stiff, narrow, grass-like leaves with pointy tips. The rosettes float to the water's surface in mid-summer, show off their white or pink-tinged flowers and then sink back to the bottom. (Zones 5–8)

Water soldier

Water Violet
American featherfoil
Hottonia species

These delicate, submerged oxygenating aquatic perennials have attractive flowers and consume excess nutrients in the pond. American featherfoil is one of the least invasive oxygenating plants, suitable for relatively small ponds and water features.

Water violet and American featherfoil grow best in **full sun** but tolerate partial shade. The soil should be a **wet, loamy** pond mix, in water 20–40 cm (8–16") deep. Use 5–20 bunches per m² (1–2 bunches for every 1–2 ft²) of water surface area. These plants produce overwintering buds that sink to the pond bottom in fall. The buds normally survive unless the pond freezes solid. If you expect your pond to do so, store the buds in a container of mud and water in a cool, frost-free location.

H. inflata (American featherfoil) forms a mass of stems with feathery foliage that spreads about 45 cm (18"). The plant remains completely submerged except for the clusters of white flowers that bloom above the surface in late spring and sometimes summer. (Zones 5–8)

H. palustris (water violet) is an indefinitely spreading, submerged plant with feathery foliage that grows 20–40 cm (8–16") tall. Clusters of white or light purple flowers are held above the water in spring and early summer. (Zones 5–8)

Yellow wax-bells

Watermint
Mentha aquatica

Watermints are versatile plants that can grow directly in the water, in a moist area next to the pond or even in a bog garden. They tolerate running water as well and can be planted in a stream or beside a waterfall, where they will trail in the flowing water.

Watermints grow well in **full sun to light shade**. The soil should be a **wet, loamy** pond mix, in water up to 10 cm (4") deep. These plants spread by long, underground shoots and may need a container or frequent pulling to control their spread. New plants can be propagated by cutting off these shoots and planting them elsewhere.

in moist soil at the pond edge or in sunken containers in the pond. Wild rice grows well from seed, often self-seeding and reappearing in following years, but it is easiest to begin with bought plants the first year.

This tall, grass-like, marginal aquatic annual can grow 2–3 m (6½–10') tall in the wild. In the home pond, it can grow 1.2–1.5 m (4–5') with a spread of 45–60 cm (18–24"). It bears flower plumes in summer, and the seeds ripen in fall. Left to naturalize, it may cover a considerable area once it establishes itself through self-seeding. (Zones 2–8)

Yellow Wax-Bells
Kirengeshoma palmata

Yellow wax-bells forms an impressive mass in a shaded spot with moist soil next to a pond, and it can also be included at the edges of a bog garden. The bright green leaves will brighten up any area. Each leaf is held firmly horizontal, separate from the leaves above and below it, producing an attractive layered look.

Yellow wax-bells grows well in **light to partial shade**. The soil should be **fertile, humus rich, acidic** and **moist**. These plants rarely needs dividing, but you can do so carefully in spring, just as the new growth begins to sprout, to propagate more plants.

This pondside perennial forms an elegant mound of lobed, maple-like leaves. It grows 60 cm–1.2 m (2–4') tall and spreads 60–90 cm (24–36"), bearing loose spikes of pale yellow flowers in late summer and fall. (Zones 5–8)

This marginal aquatic or pondside perennial grows 30–90 cm (12–36") tall and spreads 90 cm (36") or more. It is a spreading plant with upright stems that bear clusters of pinkish purple flowers at the ends of its shoots in summer. (Zones 5–8)

Wild Rice
Zizania latifolia

The height of this dramatic and elegant grass makes it a good choice for a seasonal privacy screen. Native to central and eastern Canada, it may attract wildlife to your pond.

Wild rice grows well in **full sun**. The soil should be a **fertile, wet, loamy** pond mix, in water up to 25 cm (10") deep. These plants can grow directly

Common Name	FEATURES								SEASON OF INTEREST			PLANT TYPE		
	Flowers	Foliage	Fruit/Seedheads	Oxygenating	Mini-pond	Moving Water	Still Water	Fish Habitat	Spring	Summer	Fall/Winter	Annual	Perennial	Tree/Shrub
Anacheris	•	•		•	•			•		•		•	•	
Angelica	•	•	•						•	•			•	
Arrowhead	•	•		•	•					•			•	
Astilbe	•	•	•						•	•	•		•	
Bee Balm	•									•			•	
Beech Fern		•								•			•	
Birch		•							•	•	•			•
Bladderwort	•								•	•			•	
Bleeding Heart	•	•							•	•			•	
Bog Bean	•	•			•					•			•	
Brass Buttons	•				•					•		•	•	
Buckler Fern		•								•			•	
Bugbane	•	•								•	•		•	
Bugleweed	•	•							•	•			•	
Cabomba		•		•	•		•			•		•	•	
Calla Lily	•	•			•				•	•			•	
Canadian Hemlock		•	•						•	•	•			•
Cattail	•	•	•		•			•	•	•	•		•	
Cedar		•	•						•	•	•			•
Chameleon Plant	•	•				•				•			•	
Club Rush		•	•		•		•			•	•		•	
Columbine	•	•							•	•			•	
Common Cotton Grass	•		•		•				•	•			•	
Corydalis	•	•							•	•			•	
Curled Pondweed	•	•		•	•					•		•	•	
Curly Water Thyme	•	•		•	•		•	•		•		•	•	
Daylily	•								•	•			•	
Dogweed	•	•	•						•	•	•			•
Duckweed		•			•			•		•			•	
Elephant Ears		•								•		•	•	
Eupatorium	•									•	•		•	
Fairy Moss		•			•			•		•		•	•	
Floating Heart	•	•						•	•	•	•		•	
Flowering Fern	•	•								•	•		•	

Submerged	Floating	Emergent	Marginal	Bog	Overflow	Pondside	Sun	Part Shade	Light Shade	Full Shade	ZONE	PAGE	Common Name
•	•						•				5-8	66	Anacheris
					•	•	•	•			4-8	68	Angelica
•			•				•	•			3-8	70	Arrowhead
				•	•	•		•	•		3-8	72	Astilbe
				•		•	•				3-8	74	Bee Balm
				•				•	•	•	4-8	76	Beech Fern
					•	•	•	•	•		2-8	78	Birch
	•			•			•				1-8	80	Bladderwort
						•		•	•	•	3-8	82	Bleeding Heart
		•	•	•			•				5-8	84	Bog Bean
•	•	•	•	•	•	•	•				6-8	86	Brass Buttons
				•	•	•		•	•		2-8	88	Buckler Fern
					•	•		•	•		3-8	90	Bugbane
						•		•	•	•	2-8	92	Bugleweed
•							•	•			5-8	94	Cabomba
		•	•	•	•		•				8	96	Calla Lily
						•	•	•	•	•	3-8	98	Canadian Hemlock
		•	•	•			•	•			2-8	100	Cattail
						•	•		•		2-8	102	Cedar
				•	•	•	•	•	•		4-8	104	Chameleon Plant
		•	•				•				5-8	106	Club Rush
						•		•	•		2-8	108	Columbine
		•	•	•			•				4-7	110	Common Cotton Grass
						•		•	•		3-8	112	Corydalis
•	•					•	•	•			6-8	114	Curled Pondweed
•							•				8	269	Curly Water Thyme
				•	•	•	•	•	•	•	2-8	116	Daylily
					•	•	•	•	•		2-8	118	Dogwood
	•						•	•			4-8	120	Duckweed
		•	•	•					•	•	N/H	122	Elephant Ears
				•	•	•	•	•			3-8	124	Eupatorium
	•						•	•			7-8	126	Fairy Moss
•	•						•				5-8	128	Floating Heart
				•	•	•		•	•		2-8	130	Flowering Fern

Common Name	Flowers	Foliage	Fruit/Seedheads	Oxygenating	Mini-pond	Moving Water	Still Water	Fish Habitat	Spring	Summer	Fall/Winter	Annual	Perennial	Tree/Shrub
Flowering Rush	•		•		•					•			•	
Frogbit		•			•		•			•			•	
Giant Arum	•								•	•			•	
Goat's Beard	•	•	•							•	•		•	
Golden Club	•				•	•		•	•	•			•	
Gunnera	•	•								•			•	
Hardy Calla	•	•	•							•			•	
Hornwort		•		•	•			•		•		•	•	
Horsetail		•			•	•				•			•	
Hosta	•	•								•			•	
Iris	•				•				•	•			•	
Jacob's Ladder	•	•							•	•			•	
Kaffir Lily	•										•		•	
Katsura-tree		•							•	•	•			•
Lady Fern		•								•			•	
Ligularia	•									•	•		•	
Lizard's Tail	•				•					•			•	
Lobelia	•				•					•	•		•	
Loosestrife	•	•				•				•			•	
Lotus	•	•	•		•					•			•	
Lungwort	•	•							•	•			•	
Maidenhair Fern		•								•	•		•	
Manna Grass		•	•			•		•	•	•	•		•	
Maple	•	•	•						•	•	•			•
Marsh Marigold	•					•			•				•	
Masterwort	•	•								•			•	
Meadow Rue	•	•								•			•	
Meadowsweet	•	•	•							•	•		•	
Monkey Flower	•				•					•		•		
Monkshood	•									•	•		•	
Mountain Laurel	•	•							•	•	•			•
Obedient Plant	•									•	•		•	
Ornamental Rhubarb	•	•								•			•	
Ostrich Fern		•							•	•			•	

Submerged	Floating	Emergent	Marginal	Bog	Overflow	Pondside	Sun	Part Shade	Light Shade	Full Shade	ZONE	PAGE	Common Name
			•	•			•				5-8	132	Flowering Rush
	•		•				•				5-8	134	Frogbit
			•	•	•	•	•	•			7-8	136	Giant Arum
			•	•	•			•	•	•	2-8	138	Goat's Beard
		•	•	•			•	•	•	•	5-8	140	Golden Club
			•	•	•	•	•	•	•		7-8	142	Gunnera
			•	•			•	•			3-8	144	Hardy Calla
•	•						•	•			6-8	270	Hornwort
			•	•	•	•	•				3-8	146	Horsetail
						•		•	•	•	2-8	148	Hosta
			•				•	•			2-8	150	Iris
						•		•	•		3-8	152	Jacob's Ladder
						•	•				7-8	154	Kaffir Lily
						•	•	•			4-8	156	Katsura-tree
						•		•	•	•	3-8	158	Lady Fern
				•	•	•		•	•		2-8	160	Ligularia
			•				•	•	•	•	4-8	162	Lizard's Tail
		•	•		•	•	•	•	•		4-8	164	Lobelia
						•	•	•			2-8	166	Loosestrife
		•	•				•	•			4-8	168	Lotus
					•	•		•	•	•	2-8	172	Lungwort
				•	•	•		•	•	•	2-8	174	Maidenhair Fern
		•	•				•				4-8	176	Manna Grass
						•	•	•			2-8	178	Maple
			•	•			•	•			2-8	180	Marsh Marigold
						•		•	•		4-8	182	Masterwort
				•	•	•		•	•		3-8	184	Meadow Rue
			•	•	•	•		•	•		3-8	186	Meadowsweet
			•	•	•	•		•	•		N/H	188	Monkey Flower
				•	•	•		•	•		2-8	190	Monkshood
			•	•	•	•	•	•	•		2-8	192	Mountain Laurel
				•	•	•	•	•	•		2-8	194	Obedient Plant
				•	•	•	•	•			3-8	196	Ornamental Rhubarb
					•	•		•	•	•	1-8	198	Ostrich Fern

Common Name	Flowers	Foliage	Fruit/Seedheads	Oxygenating	Mini-pond	Moving Water	Still Water	Fish Habitat	Spring	Summer	Fall/Winter	Annual	Perennial	Tree/Shrub
	FEATURES								SEASON OF INTEREST			PLANT TYPE		
Papyrus	•	•	•		•	•				•			•	
Parrot Feather		•		•	•	•		•		•		•	•	
Pennywort		•			•	•		•		•			•	
Periwinkle	•	•			•	•		•		•			•	
Pickerel Weed	•	•			•	•		•		•			•	
Pitcher Plant	•	•							•	•			•	
Plume Poppy	•	•	•							•	•		•	
Pondweed	•	•		•	•			•		•		•	•	
Primrose	•					•			•	•			•	
Ribbon Grass		•	•					•		•	•		•	
Rodgersia	•		•							•	•		•	
Rush		•	•		•	•				•			•	
Salvinia		•			•		•	•		•		•	•	
Sedge	•	•	•		•					•	•		•	
Shield Fern		•								•	•		•	
Silver Grass		•	•							•	•		•	
Spearwort	•	•		•	•	•		•		•			•	
Spike Rush		•	•	•	•	•				•	•		•	
Swamp Hibiscus	•		•							•	•		•	
Sweet Flag		•			•	•		•		•	•		•	
Tape Grass	•			•	•			•		•		•	•	
Thalia	•	•						•		•		•	•	
Turtle Head	•									•	•		•	
Umbrella Plant	•	•			•				•	•			•	
Valerian	•		•							•			•	
Virginia Bluebells	•					•			•				•	
Water Forget-me-not	•				•	•			•	•		•	•	
Water Hyacinth	•	•		•	•			•		•	•	•	•	
Water Lettuce		•			•		•	•		•		•	•	
Water Lily	•	•			•		•	•		•	•		•	
Water Poppy	•	•			•		•	•		•		•	•	
Watercress	•	•			•	•			•	•	•		•	
Willow		•							•	•	•			•
Wood Rush	•	•	•			•				•	•		•	
Yellow Pond Lily	•	•					•	•		•			•	

Submerged	Floating	Emergent	Marginal	Bog	Overflow	Pondside	Sun	Part Shade	Light Shade	Full Shade	ZONE	PAGE	Common Name
			•				•	•			6-8	200	Papyrus
•		•					•				5-8	202	Parrot Feather
			•	•		•	•	•			4-8	204	Pennywort
					•	•		•	•	•	3-8	206	Periwinkle
			•	•			•	•			4-8	208	Pickerel Weed
				•			•				2-8	210	Pitcher Plant
					•	•	•				3-8	212	Plume Poppy
•							•				5-8	271	Pondweed
			•		•	•		•	•		4-8	214	Primrose
			•	•	•	•	•	•			2-8	216	Ribbon Grass
					•	•		•	•		3-8	218	Rodgersia
			•	•	•		•	•			4-8	220	Rush
	•						•				N/H	222	Salvinia
		•	•	•	•	•	•	•			3-8	224	Sedge
					•	•		•	•	•	3-8	226	Shield Fern
						•	•				3-8	228	Silver Grass
•	•	•	•	•			•	•			5-8	230	Spearwort
•			•				•	•			3-8	232	Spike Rush
			•	•	•	•	•				4-8	234	Swamp Hibiscus
		•	•	•			•				4-8	236	Sweet Flag
•							•	•			8	272	Tape Grass
			•				•				5-8	238	Thalia
						•	•	•			3-8	240	Turtle Head
			•	•	•		•				5-8	242	Umbrella Plant
					•	•	•		•		2-8	244	Valerian
					•	•			•	•	3-8	246	Virginia Bluebells
			•	•	•			•			3-8	248	Water Forget-me-not
•	•		•				•				N/H	250	Water Hyacinth
	•		•				•	•			N/H	252	Water Lettuce
•	•						•				4-8	254	Water Lily
•	•						•				N/H	258	Water Poppy
			•	•	•		•	•	•		4-8	260	Watercress
						•	•				2-8	262	Willow
			•	•	•		•	•	•	•	4-8	264	Wood Rush
•	•						•				3-8	266	Yellow Pond Lily

Glossary

Acid soil: soil with a pH lower than 7.0

Aerobic: living or occurring only in the presence of oxygen

Alkaline soil: soil with a pH higher than 7.0

Anaerobic: living or occurring in an environment without oxygen

Annual: a plant that germinates, flowers, sets seeds and dies in one growing season

Basal leaves: leaves that form from the crown, at the base of the plant

Berm: a mound of earth, or earth and debris

Bog plant: a plant that thrives in wet soil

Bract: a special, modified leaf located at the base of a flower or inflorescence. Bracts may be small or large, green or coloured

Crown: the part of the plant at or just below soil level where the shoots join the roots

Cultivar: a cultivated plant variety with one or more distinct differences from the species, e.g., in flower colour or disease resistance

Deadhead: removing spent flowers to maintain a neat appearance and encourage a long blooming season

Direct sow: to sow seeds directly into the garden

Dormancy: a period of plant inactivity, usually during winter or unfavourable conditions

Double flower: a flower with an unusually large number of petals

Emergent: a plant that grows in deep water, with its stems, leaves and flowers above the water surface and its roots below

Genus: a category of biological classification between the species and family levels; the first word in a scientific name indicates the genus

Hardy: capable of surviving unfavourable conditions, such as cold weather or frost, without protection

Humus: decomposed or decomposing organic material in the soil

Hybrid: a plant resulting from natural or human-induced cross-breeding between varieties, species or genera

Invasive: able to spread aggressively from the planting site and outcompete others

Loam: a loose soil composed of clay, sand and organic matter, often highly fertile

Marginal: a plant that grows in shallow water, with its stems, leaves and flowers above the water surface and its leaves below

Oxygenator: a submerged plant that releases oxygen into the water and reduces algae growth in the pond

Perennial: a plant that takes three or more years to complete its life cycle

Plantlet: a young or small plant

pH: a measure of acidity or alkalinity; soil pH influences availability of nutrients for plants

Pondside: The transition area between the pond and the rest of the garden. A pondside plant likes moist but well-drained soil.

Rhizome: a root-like, food-storing stem that grows horizontally at or just below soil level, from which new shoots may emerge

Rosette: a low, flat cluster of leaves arranged like the petals of a rose

Seedhead: dried, inedible fruit that contains seeds

Self-seeding: reproducing by means of seeds without human assistance, so that new plants constantly replace those that die

Single flower: a flower with a single ring of typically four or five petals

Spathe: A leaf-like bract that encloses a flower cluster or spike

Species: the fundamental unit of biological classification; the entity from which cultivars and varieties are derived

Submerged: a plant that grows under water

Tender: incapable of surviving the climatic conditions of a given region and requiring protection from frost or cold

Variegation: foliage that has more than one colour, often patched, striped or bearing leaf margins of a different colour

Variety: a naturally occurring variant of a species

Index of Plant Names

Entries in **bold** type indicate the main plant headings.

Anacheris

Bog Bean

Calla Lily

Daylily

Floating Heart

Giant Arum

Iris

Lotus

Marsh Marigold

Water Garden Plants for Canada
Photo Credits
Aquascape Designs 34, 53; **Alan Bibby** 37b, 66, 94, 202, 270, 271, 272; **Rowena Burns** 141; **Karen Carriere** 235a, 235b; **Joan de Grey** 196; **Tamara Eder** 31a, 31c, 43, 55, 56, 58, 75b, 83a, 93b, 97b, 102, 108, 109a, 112, 113a, 113b, 117a, 138, 143b, 149a, 152, 160, 161b, 165a, 165b, 166, 167a, 179b, 180, 181a, 181b, 184, 188, 189a, 189b, 190, 191b, 212, 213a, 218, 234, 243a, 243b; 248; **Elliot Engley** 46a; **Derek Fell** 31d, 76, 77a, 77b, 81b, 90, 110, 111b, 137b, 140, 177b, 211, 245b, 247b, 260, 261a, 261b, 265a, 268-269a, 285c; **Erika Flatt** 13, 14b, 17b, 17c, 22a, 24b, 25a, 25b, 26a, 26b, 26c, 27a, 29a, 38, 46b, 47a, 47b, 54a, 59, 61, 71b, 84, 93a, 97a, 126, 127b, 144, 147b, 162, 198, 200, 201b, 205b, 208, 220, 221b, 222, 223a, 223b, 225a, 250, 253a, 262; **Liza Fleming** 81a, 86, 87b, 133a, 134, 135, 145b, 267a, 269b; **Anne Gordon** 89b, 197a, 244; **James A. Gordon** 136; **Linda Kershaw** 118; **Liz Klose** 131a, 131b, 225b, 229b; **Dawn Loewen** 103b; **Janet Loughrey** 124, 197b, 210, 274-275; **Tim Matheson** 31b, 45a, 45b, 45c, 48a, 48b, 48c, 48d, 48e, 57, 72, 73a, 73b, 74, 75a, 78, 79a, 79b, 82, 98, 99a, 99b, 103a, 116, 148, 150, 153a, 156, 157a, 157b, 164, 172, 173a, 173b, 187b, 191a, 192, 193a, 193b, 194, 195a, 195b, 206, 207a, 207b, 215a, 236, 237b, 249a; **Moore Water Gardens** 42; **Kim O'Leary** 1, 142, 143a, 154, 155a, 155b; **Allison Penko** 3, 4, 12, 14a, 17a, 20, 21, 27c, 28, 29b, 30a, 30b, 32, 35a, 37a, 49, 50, 51, 52, 54b, 64, 67, 69, 70, 71a, 85a, 89a, 91a, 91b, 95a, 95b, 100, 101a, 104, 105a, 105b, 106, 107a, 107b, 114, 115a, 115b, 117b, 119b, 120, 121a, 121b, 123a, 123b, 125a, 128, 129a, 129b, 139a, 145a, 146, 147a, 149b, 151a, 151b, 159b, 161a, 163a, 168, 169a, 169b, 170a, 170b, 171a, 171b, 175a, 175b, 176, 177a, 178, 201a, 203a, 203b, 204, 205a, 209a, 209b, 215b, 217a, 217b, 219a, 221a, 224, 228, 230, 231a, 231b, 232, 233a, 233b, 237a, 238, 239a, 239b, 240, 241a, 241b, 241c, 249b, 251a, 251b, 252, 253b, 254, 255a, 255b, 256a, 256b, 257a, 257b, 258, 259a, 259b, 263a, 273; **Laura Peters** 18, 19, 22b, 24a, 27b, 35b, 40, 41a, 41b, 63, 65, 85b, 88, 92, 101b, 119a, 122, 127a, 130, 153b, 158, 159a, 163b, 167b, 174, 179a, 182, 183a, 183b, 187a, 199a, 199b, 213b, 216, 219b, 226, 227a, 229a, 242, 263b; **Robert Ritchie** 60, 62, 109b, 125b; **Leila Sidi** 214; **Peter Thompstone** 83b, 139b, 186; **Mark Turner** 80, 87a, 111a, 132, 133b, 137a, 227b, 245a, 246, 247a, 264, 265b, 266, 267b; **The Bloomin Bog** 16, 33, 39, 44; **Valleybrook Gardens** 185a, 185b; **Don Williamson** 68, 96